simply™

Native American astrology

DEBORAH DURBIN

A Sterling / Zambezi Book
Sterling Publishing Co., Inc.
New York

Library of Congress Cataloging-in-Publication Data Available

2 4 6 8 10 9 7 5 3 1

Published in 2007 by Sterling Publishing Co., Inc.
387 Park Avenue South, New York, NY 10016
©2006 by Deborah Durbin
Published and distributed in the United Kingdom solely by
Zambezi Publishing, Ltd.
P.O. Box 221, Plymouth, Devon PL2 2EQ
www.zampub.com
Distributed in Canada by Sterling Publishing
℅ Canadian Manda Group, 165 Dufferin Street
Toronto, Ontario, Canada M6K 3H6
Distributed in Australia by Capricorn Link (Australia) Pty. Ltd.
P.O. Box 704, Windsor, NSW 2756, Australia

Printed in China
All rights reserved

Zambezi ISBN-13: 978-1-903065-52-5
ISBN-10: 903065-52-6
Sterling ISBN-13: 978-1-4027-2697-2
ISBN-10: 1-4027-2697-X

For information about custom editions, special sales, premium and
corporate purchases, please contact Sterling Special Sales
Department at 800-805-5489 or specialsales@sterlingpub.com.

contents

1

HISTORY AND INTRODUCTION

The modern image often conjured up when we speak of Native Americans is one of a wise old man with a colorful headdress made from eagle feathers, sitting on the top of a mountain, calmly smoking his peace pipe. However, the Native American culture is far more complex than the media would have us believe . . .

Migration from Asia

The earliest inhabitants of the Americas most likely migrated from the continent of Asia across the Bering Strait land bridge to what is now known as Alaska, at some time in the past, possibly during the last glacial period. Over the course of many years, they migrated southward throughout what is now known as the United States, as well as to Central and South America and throughout Canada.

Once established, and over time, the natives ranged from the Inuit and Eskimo in the north to the inhabitants of Tierra del Fuego in the far south, and all the lands between, including the Caribbean islands and the jungles of South America. In short, the natives of the Americas became very successful in terms of survival and adaptation to their various environments.

Since the arrival of Europeans on the North and South American continents just over five hundred years ago, some native peoples have managed to survive, while others have been completely destroyed. Others have intermingled with Spanish, Portuguese, Europeans, or black Africans who were imported as slaves.

In North America and Canada, the indigenous peoples are known as Native Americans and Native Canadians, respectively. In Central and South America, there were once Toltec, Mayan, and Aztec, among many other peoples, so the variation among the remaining groups is immense, their development is varied, and each group has its own traditions, beliefs, religions, and attitudes.

TRIBES

Just as there are many, many different cultures and groups of people, there are many different tribes of Native Americans. The following is a small list of just a few of the many tribes that still exist today:

Native Canadians	Native Americans
Beaver Lake Tribe	Abenaki
Chippewa	Alabama Quassarte
Fort Hope	Arapaho
Haida	Blackfeet
Innu	Cherokee
Manitoba	Cheyenne
Mi'kmaq	Choctaw
Nunavut	Comanche
Oujé-Bougoumou Cree	Crow
Siksika	Flathead
The Six Nations of the	Mashantucket Pequot
Iroquois	Mohawk
T'sou-Ke	Navajo
	Pawnee
	Quinault
	Sioux
	Spokane
	Tonkawa
	Washoe
	Wichita

There are many more tribes still in existence today, and a simple Internet search will provide you with information about them.

ASTROLOGY

Every culture on Earth has a link to the invention of some form of astrology and various forms of calendar. Babylonian astrology led to Egyptian astrology, which was later refined by the Greeks and Romans. This form of astrology gave us our familiar signs of the zodiac and the Western system as we know it today. Other cultures linked times of the year to the creatures that they hunted or to those that were known to be dangerous to the inhabitants of their lands.

Native peoples the world over observed animals and plants in ways that we have long since forgotten. For instance, we might consider the butterfly to be a strange astrological symbol, but the appearance of an abundance of butterflies probably heralds a good crop of something that humans can eat-perhaps some early green vegetable or salad item. Native Americans have always been people of the land rather than city dwellers, so it is not surprising that the animals related to the seasons and areas in which they lived have become part of their astrology.

Over the millennia, there must have been many hundreds of forms of Native American calendar, millions of different religious beliefs, and just as many different astrological outlooks. Now what is known as "medicine wheel astrology" has become associated with Native Americans, but even so, the system has not yet set itself in stone, so there are still variations on the basic theme.

In this book, we look at the medicine wheel concept and give you information that you can work with, and then we look at totem animals and show you how to find your main one and important subsidiary ones.

As the title suggests, you do not need to know about birth charts, Moon signs, and Sun signs, nor do you need any prior knowledge of astrology to be successful with this book. Simply read on and enjoy your journey into the world of Native American astrology.

2

THE MEDICINE WHEEL

The word "medicine" is a misnomer in this context, because in the world of Native American astrology, it has nothing to do with doctors or remedies. It actually refers more closely to the concept of "putting things into order and creating harmony," in this case, incorporating a kind of yin and yang or *I Ching* concept of the natural order of everything. The confusion with the concepts of harmony, mending, and healing probably was created when white men tried to learn native languages. That said, the very term "medicine wheel" implies a concept that could never be taken from anything other than Native American thought, so it carries a romance all its own and is the perfect name for its purpose.

It is possible that the medicine wheel is based on some early Chinese system. As we saw in the introduction, the early

Wheel as Measuring Instrument

Native Americans migrated from Asia during the last ice age, if not earlier, and we know that early forms of the *I Ching* and feng shui go back that far. The second possibility is that the similarities are just coincidence. After all, most early systems used a circle, and all were concerned with the calendar and with compass directions. As with many other early forms of astrology, astronomy, and measurements of time and dates—Stonehenge included—the wheel is a very basic and ancient form of measuring instrument.

THE WORLD.

As with Chinese and other systems, the medicine wheel pinpoints the seasons and also refers to the stages of life.

In Western astrology, the cardinal signs of Aries, Cancer, Libra, and Capricorn mark the times of the year when each new season begins, while the fixed signs of Taurus, Leo, Scorpio, and Aquarius mark the midpoint of each season. The fixed signs frequently appear in ancient astrology illustrations, often with the sign of Scorpio depicted by its old symbol, the eagle. Even the ceiling of the church in the Vatican shows these four seasonal symbols, as does the World card in the Rider-Waite tarot deck.

Native American astrology also uses the images of creatures to depict the seasons. These creatures exist in *addition* to the twelve "zodiac" signs of the medicine wheel. They mark the turning point of each season and also the turning points during each day (dawn, noon, dusk, midnight). The four "seasonal" creatures are the white buffalo, the golden eagle, the coyote, and the grizzly bear.

In Western astrology, each of the twelve astrological signs belongs to one of the four elements, which rotate through the signs.

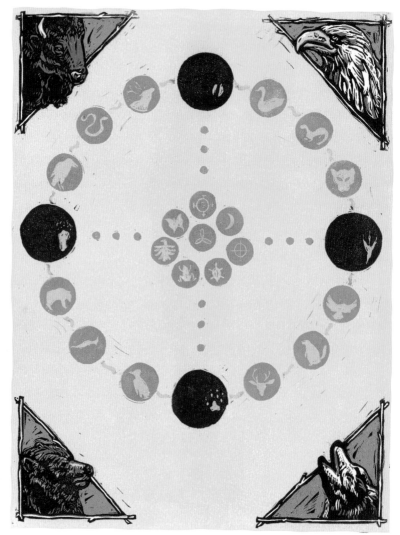

Medicine Wheel with Seasons

Western Astrology System

ZODIAC SIGN	ELEMENT	ZODIAC SIGN	ELEMENT
Aries	Fire	Libra	Air
Taurus	Earth	Scorpio	Water
Gemini	Air	Sagittarius	Fire
Cancer	Water	Capricorn	Earth
Leo	Fire	Aquarius	Air
Virgo	Earth	Pisces	Water

In Native American astrology, each sign belongs to a clan, which rotates through the system in a similar manner.

Native American Astrology System

ZODIAC SIGN	CLAN	ZODIAC SIGN	CLAN
Snow goose	Turtle	Flicker	Frog
Otter	Butterfly	Sturgeon	Thunderbird
Cougar	Frog	Grizzly bear	Turtle
Red hawk	Thunderbird	Raven	Butterfly
Beaver	Turtle	Snake	Frog
Deer	Butterfly	Elk	Thunderbird

Here is the medicine wheel with all the signs in place, along with the clans and seasonal animal totems.

Some Native Americans still use the agricultural calendar invented by the Aztecs, and others use a lunar calendar. This has now been incorporated into the "calendar month" design of the medicine wheel, which has since been aligned, more or less, with the dates used in Western astrology.

The twelve Moons correspond to the weather or activities that one would expect to occur during each season. Each astrological sign also corresponds to a tree, a stone, and a color.

A PROFUSION AND CONFUSION OF NAMES

The animal names vary within Native American astrology systems. For instance, the sign that some tribes call the sturgeon is known as the salmon by other tribes.

Dates, Signs, Moons, and Correspondences

Date	Moon	Sign	Plant	Stone/Metal	Clan	Color
December 22-January 19	Earth	Snow goose	Birch tree	Quartz	Turtle	White
January 20-February 18	Rest and cleansing	Otter	Aspen	Silver	Butterfly	Silver
February 19-March 20	Big winds	Cougar	Plantain	Turquoise	Frog	Turquoise
March 21-April 19	Budding trees	Red hawk	Dandelion	Fire opal	Thunderbird	Yellow
April 20-May 20	Frogs return	Beaver	Blue camas	Chrysocolla	Turtle	Blue
May 21-June 20	Corn planting	Deer	Yarrow	Moss agate	Butterfly	Pale green
June 21-July 22	Strong Sun	Flicker	Wild rose	Carnelian	Frog	Pink
July 23-August 22	Ripe berries	Sturgeon	Raspberry	Garnet	Thunderbird	Red
August 23-September 22	Harvest	Grizzly bear	Violet	Amethyst	Turtle	Purple
September 23-October 23	Ducks fly	Raven	Mullein	Jasper	Butterfly	Brown
October 24-November 21	Freeze up	Snake	Thistle	Malachite	Frog	Orange
November 22-December 21	Long snows	Elk	Spruce	Obsidian	Thunderbird	Black

3

THE NORTH

Main totem animal	Waboose (white buffalo)
Subsidiary totem animals	Moose, bear
Direction	North
Season	Winter
Time	After midnight
Weather	Very cold
Age group	Old age
Activity	Rest, repairs, recovery, and love making
Mineral	Alabaster
Element	Earth
Plant	Sweetgrass

THE NORTH PART OF THE MEDICINE WHEEL

North Part of Medicine Wheel

The most commonly mentioned animal totem representing the north is the white buffalo, or the waboose, which is connected to the element of earth. Other animals representing the north are the moose and bear. All these animals inhabit the north and are well adapted for life in a cold climate—or for hibernating in one during the worst of the winter. They each develop layers of fat to see them through the winter; they move slowly, sleep a lot, and forage when times are good. They have adapted to their environment. The earth element also represents slow movement, steadfastness, reliability, and obstinacy. The earth can move with great force during an avalanche or earthquake or when a volcano erupts, but it is normally static and unchanging.

In the case of the buffalo and moose, they provided meat, skin, bone for tools, fat, and sustenance for the Stone Age natives of the Americas before the coming of the dubious benefits of civilization. In rural communities, the winter is a time for mending tools and equipment and for replacing worn-out items. It is also a time to spend with one's family or tribe. Most traditions light beacons and say prayers at the solstice in the hope that the Sun will not forget to come around again.

The winter is the most paradoxical time of the medicine wheel. It is a time when things appear to be dormant, and yet some of the deepest growth is occurring. It is the time when seeds lie frozen and take in all the Earth's energy to allow them to grow in the seasons that follow. The time of the waboose is a time for slowing down and taking things easy. It is a time for peace, forgiveness, and compassion for all who are around you.

One of the gifts the waboose can give us is an intuitive understanding. It gives us psychic abilities and meaningful dreams. The white buffalo is an animal that gave up everything for the native peoples. It is the white buffalo woman who gave the pipe of peace to the people. During the times of the Spirit Keeper of the North, it is beneficial to contemplate your life and think about questions of life and the hereafter. It is a time of patience and peace, and you may feel more psychic at this time than at others.

Other winter pastimes are hunting and fishing. This is partly because the tribe still needs protein to see it through the cold winter, and the inhabitants of the tribe will spend time drying, salting, or otherwise preserving food to carry their group through the lean times. Even now that many human beings have lived in civilized societies for upward of ten thousand years, it is still a fact that fewer babies are born at the start of winter. This goes for both hemispheres and every kind of society. The majority of babies come into the world during spring, summer, and autumn, when there is plenty of nourishment for the mother. Thus the quiet time is a great opportunity for couples to snuggle up, keep warm, and make love.

The mineral associated with the waboose is alabaster, which is commonly a white or yellow stone with brown hues. Soft alabaster has been carved for centuries into pipes that tribesmen have blown to call their herds. Images of such pipes have been found on early Egyptian tombs, and there they represent the flower of youth. Egypt might seem to be a long way from the Native American culture, but remember that Thor Heyerdahl's expeditions appear to indicate that it was possible for the ancient Egyptians to have made the journey across the Atlantic in papyrus boats. We also know that the central and southern Aztec and Mayan civilizations still have some influence over Native American thinking, so it is not such a leap of the imagination to see how these ideas might have been transmitted through the Americas over time.

Alabaster encourages us to understand that there is great strength in gentleness. If you were born anywhere between December 22 and March 20, you should carry a piece of alabaster with you to create a sense of peace and serenity around you.

The plant associated with the Spirit Keeper of the North is the sweetgrass. It is widely believed to be the plant from which all others have grown, so it is also known as "hair of the mother." Sweetgrass carries a deep wisdom of the Earth and draws positive energies when it is burned. Those who burn it for smudging purposes believe that it calls good spirits to the person using it.

Sweetgrass is a perennial that can be found near wet areas, and it grows in long, reedlike strands. It is often woven into thick braids for use in smudging. Native Americans would call on the Spirit Keeper of the North when smoking sweetgrass. Sometimes they give it as gifts to their relatives.

The time associated with the north angle of the medicine wheel is after midnight, when the world rests and dreams. The season is winter and the age group is the elderly. Some modern astrologers ascribe the north to the element of earth.

4

THE EAST

Main totem animal	Wabun (golden eagle)
Subsidiary totem animals	Hummingbird, owl, hawk
Direction	East
Season	Spring
Time	Sunrise and early morning
Weather	Changeable
Age group	Youth
Activity	Planting, young animals, fresh starts
Mineral	Catlinite
Element	Air
Plant	Tobacco

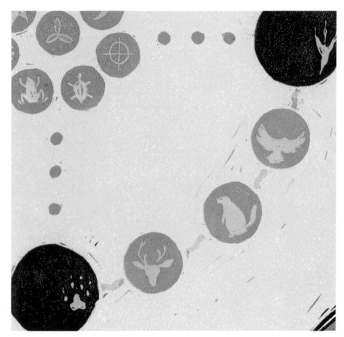

*East Part of
Medicine Wheel*

The major totem animal that is associated with the east is the golden eagle, or wabun. Other animals associated with the east are the hummingbird, the owl, and the hawk. These bird associations give us an image of something that is free of attachment to the Earth and able to fly above this side of the medicine wheel.

As far as timing is concerned, this area represents the rising of the Sun and the early morning, and the time of the year for the east is spring. The symbolism here is of birth, young animals, new beginnings, and the optimism that one displays when planting new crops. The time is also symbolic of youth.

When the Earth enters this time of the year, all life seems to be bursting forth with new energy. Many of the animals bear their young and begin to teach them to survive in the big, wide world. When humans are in the time of the wabun, they are also busy, like the rest of nature. This is a magical time for both animal and human, when anything seems possible. It's an ideal time to experience life and to try out new ideas. Perhaps those things you've only dreamt about can become real possibilities during this time of the year, and this encourages you to do something new. If you were born during this time of the year, then you are in a better position than most for creating new opportunities for yourself.

Some of the most important lessons you can learn from the east are how to turn the knowledge of the spirit world into the knowledge of our everyday world. This side of the medicine wheel encourages you to be open to new ideas and to have the courage to go out and get what you want. It is a time for new growth and energy. The mineral associated with the eagle is catlinite, and the color associated with this magnificent eagle is gold. The eagle is seen as being all-powerful among birds, and it represents new beginnings, enthusiasm, and creativity.

Modern astrologers associate this area of the wheel with the element of air. All forms of astrology see air as an element of communication and movement. Air is rarely still for long; it moves the clouds around and brings rain or freshness to the land. A little rain is needed if crops are to grow and if people and animals are to have clean water for drinking and washing. The birds that form the totem animals for this part of the medicine wheel rely upon the "solidity" of the air element to keep them flying—and thus able to feed themselves and their families.

If you were born anywhere between March 21 and June 20, then the wabun, Spirit Keeper of the East, is your spirit keeper. The wabun brings the eternal promise of spring and helps us to understand that there will always be new beginnings. The gifts from the wabun are those of spontaneity, playfulness, wonder, inquisitiveness, and the ability to explore new things.

The tobacco plant is the plant associated with the Spirit Keeper of the East, and although the use of tobacco is now frowned upon in Western society, many Native American people worship this plant. They believe tobacco to be an herb that is one of the most sacred of their plants; when smoked in sacred spirit, tobacco is offered to the spirit keeper and spirit guides. The tobacco plant that we refer to has leaves that are six to twelve inches long. Smoking this plant is not the same as buying a packet of chemical-filled cigarettes. Native Americans use this plant as a smudge to clear an area of bad air or bad influences, or they use it in a pipe to promote peace and growth.

NOTE:

This is not an endorsement to take up smoking!

The time associated with this direction is sunrise and, unsurprisingly, the age group is youth.

5

THE SOUTH

Main totem animal	Shawnodese (coyote)
Subsidiary totem animals	Lion, wolf
Direction	South
Season	Summer
Time	Noon
Weather	Very hot
Age group	Young adulthood
Activity	Sex, passion, birth, hunting, fighting
Mineral	Serpentine
Element	Fire
Plant	Sage bush

South Part of the Medicine Wheel

The animal totem for the south is the coyote, or shawnodese; the lion and the wolf are secondary totems. These animals are successful predators who can hunt alone, although they do often hunt in packs. The representative ideas linked to the south are sex and passion, early adulthood, and a time when one has the strength to fight an enemy, to hunt for food, or to give birth and look after a family. Naturally, at this time the crops are growing vigorously and some are ready to eat. There are plenty of animals around to hunt, and these provide immediate nourishment, skins, tools, and food that can be dried for future use. The symbolism associated with this time is pride and plenty.

The time that this direction represents is midday, and the season is the summer. Modern astrologers link this direction to the element of fire. Symbolically speaking, fire is associated with enthusiasm and with the fun and pleasure that one can get from any activity. For instance, a group of men hunting in packs can have a wonderful day out. However, their pleasure is also useful because—ideally—they come back at the end of the trip laden with ducks, beavers, antelope, buffalo, fish, or anything else that will keep the tribe fed, clothed, and happy. This element is also associated with passion and lovemaking, which themselves are keys to the future survival of any tribe—apart from being very enjoyable activities.

If you were born anywhere between June 21 and September 22, the shawnodese is your spirit keeper. This is a time of self-assurance and open and energetic activity. It is a time of learning new things and of improving oneself. To many native peoples, the shawnodese is seen as a trickster in the most powerful sense. To others he is a form of the Creator. He has a very powerful presence, and he creates a time to explore new things and new emotions.

The mineral represented by the shawnodese is serpentine, which rests beneath much of North America. It has a greasy or waxy texture and contains the colors yellow, black, green, brown, and white, or a mixture of all these colors. It is thought to heal a serpent's bite and has been used by native peoples throughout the Americas for making objects such as jewelry, carvings, and pipe bowls. Some traditions state that serpentine can be used to prevent one from being bitten or stung by spiders and snakes. Even though it has been used for thousands of years, to those who collect crystals, serpentine is still considered fairly new, and like the shawnodese, it brings an air of mystery with it.

The plant associated with the Spirit Keeper of the South is the sagebrush plant, which is simply known as sage. This plant grows in many forms and is sometimes confused with culinary sage. A shrub with slender branches that can grow from two to four feet in length, this sage produces tiny purplish flowers and grows wild in drier climates such as California. The most important use of this sage is as a smudge, because it helps to transform nonworking energies into working energies. When burnt, sage emits a pungent, strong, thick smoke and helps to cleanse or transform everything in its path.

The time associated with this part of the wheel is noon, and the age group is adulthood.

6

THE WEST

Main totem animal	Mudieneewis (grizzly bear)
Subsidiary totem animals	Beaver, snake
Direction	West
Season	Autumn
Time	Sunset
Weather	Cooling down, changeable
Age-group	Maturity, middle age
Activity	Harvest
Mineral	Soapstone
Element	Water
Plant	Cedar tree

*West Part of
Medicine Wheel*

The main animal totem for this direction is the grizzly bear, or mudieneewis. Other animals linked to the west are the beaver and the snake. The bear and beaver prepare for winter by catching fish and storing up body fat, while the snake can become as deeply lethargic as a hibernating bear when conditions demand. The snake can also shed its skin when starting to outgrow it.

In rural terms, the autumn is a time of harvest, of bottling and preserving fruits and vegetables, of drying animal flesh and making pemmican and jerky, and of preparing for the coming winter. Families and villagers work together in a productive manner, and they come together in prayer to give thanks when they have finished. The season for this part of the wheel is the autumn and the time is sunset. In life this direction represents vigorous and experienced middle age.

Modern astrologers ascribe this area to the element of water. Water is strange, because it can appear to be docile, but as we have seen from the recent tsunamis and floods, at times it can be the most dangerous of all the elements. It covers large areas of the Earth's surface. Like all other elements, water is necessary to life and carries most of the world's plant and animal life beneath its surface. Rivers were the traditional routes for travel, trading, and transportation, especially in wet and muddy weather, and many Native American tribes have used dugouts, canoes, and inshore ships to move themselves and their trade goods from one place to another. Choose a mature person with plenty of experience to lead such an expedition.

If you were born anywhere between September 23 and December 21, then the Spirit Keeper of the West is your spirit keeper. At this time of the year, seeds fall back into the ground and everything begins to slow down. Once the harvest is safely in and the food, skins, and other implements are correctly prepared, the tribe can slowly start to wind down to winter and to relax.

The grizzly bear is one of the strongest and most intelligent creatures on Earth, a fabulous problem solver. When people reach this time of the year, they feel that they have established themselves. This is a good time to look within yourself and to gain strength from your past achievements, and also to reflect on what you have achieved during the past year. This is a powerful time when one can reassess one's needs.

The plant associated with this sign is the cedar tree. This strong plant houses and nurtures the Earth's children. Use cedar with sage and sweetgrass as a smudge to take away the burdens of living, and refresh and promote new life.

The mineral linked to this sign is soapstone. Soapstone is often found in Norway and Canada. It has a greasy, soft texture, which appears dull or pearly and varies in color from pale green to black, gray, or white. Through the ages, refreshing powders and bath products have been made from its main ingredient, and it has also been used for carvings, jewelry, and pipes. Soapstone helps with strengthening on all levels—spiritual, emotional, mental, and physical. It also wards off illness by cleansing. Soapstone is considered to strengthen the immune system and can be used like soap to wash and clean.

The time associated with this direction is sunset, and the age group is middle age.

7

PUTTING THINGS TOGETHER

Although Native American astrology is not particularly predictive, one can see how it can easily be used as an oracle, so if you'd like to try your hand at this, here are some ideas.

Create an illustration to represent the four quadrants of the medicine wheel. Place your illustration on the ground. Now focus on whatever is bothering you and ask your spiritual guide to give you a sensible and useful answer. Your question might relate to love and relationships, health, money, work, and so on. Now gently drop or throw small pebbles or shells onto the design and note the way that the stones or shells have landed. The oracle will show you what you should do, how you should do it, the time when things will come to pass, and where to look for luck in the future.

Four Quadrants of Medicine Wheel

For example, if a modern querent were to ask when he or she would find a new job, and the shells or stones landed on the northern part of the quadrant wheel, this would show the querent that he or she would be successful in the winter, should go to the north, and should ensure that all his or her tools (or qualifications, perhaps) were ready and in place. If the querent wanted to know the most propitious time to go for an interview, this reading really is not very helpful, as the north quadrant refers to the time around and after midnight. In this case, it is better to do a second reading with one pebble or shell. If the timing still comes up as impractical, then the choice is obviously out of the querent's hands, and he or she must simply take the interview at the time that the interviewer (or fate) considers the most convenient.

In another possible scenario, the querent is not sure whether his or her lover is "the one." The querent has a feeling that the lover just cannot be trusted to provide the emotional and practical security he or she needs—especially if the querent wishes to start a family. The majority of pebbles and shells tossed into the quadrant illustration fall in the east. This shows that the querent's lover is indeed immature and that the lover's role in the querent's life is to open the querent's eyes to the many possibilities that can come through loving contact with others. This lover may not stick around in the way that the querent would like. If the querent wants to know when this affair will end or when a new one will start, it will be in the spring.

If you use a bit of imagination, you could offer a second reading to show whether the querent's true love will be younger or older and what character he or she will have— for instance, a hardworking salesperson (hunter), a steady, reliable type (farmer), or a passionate fly-by-night. The possibilities are endless!

8

THE SNOW GOOSE
December 22 – January 19

Clan	*Turtle*
Spirit keeper	*Spirit Keeper of the North*
Moon	*Earth-renewal Moon*
Crystal or mineral	*Quartz*
Tree or plant	*Birch tree*
Color	*White*

INTRODUCING THE ANIMAL SIGNS

As we mentioned in Chapter 2, "The Medicine Wheel," the Native American medicine wheel is divided up into twelve signs, just as in modern Western astrology. However, instead of the modern animals that make up the Western astrological star signs, Native Americans use the animals that we showed in the table "Native American Astrology System" in Chapter 2. Fortunately, modern astrologers in the Native American tradition have aligned the two systems so that they match. For example, if you were born on January 10, you would be a Capricorn in Western astrology, and your Native American sign would be the snow goose.

So now let us move on to explore each zodiac sign in the Native American astrological system, along with the traits and information carried for that particular sign.

THE EARTH-RENEWAL MOON

The earth-renewal Moon begins at the time of the winter solstice in the northern hemisphere, when the Sun starts to turn northward once again and begins to bring warmth that quickens growth in the earth. This Moon teaches you to be as clear a receiver and transmitter of universal energy and as clear a communicator of the ancient knowledge as the birch tree. This process teaches you to be fluid and flexible, yet clear, prudent, and wise. People born under this sign have keen vision and can easily deal with individuals from all backgrounds and walks of life.

THE SNOW GOOSE

The snow goose, a white bird, has been called "the goose from beyond the north wind" because of its migration in the spring. Some species of snow goose travel five thousand miles each year. The snow goose is very gregarious, so it is not unusual to see twenty or thirty thousand birds resting in one location. At nesting grounds the young geese show respect for tradition by allowing older birds to have the first choice of sites. Both goose and gander stay with their eggs. Snow geese like everything to be perfect; they are literal nitpickers! They will spend hours happily picking mosquitoes from under their feathers. People born under the sign of the snow goose are perfectionists!

THE BIRCH TREE

The birch tree is one of the most ancient and abundant trees. Native peoples utilized its bark and leaves for teas and medicinal remedies. Branches of the birch can be bound together and used to help the body expel toxins. Birch makes a good tea for the treatment of skin conditions, digestive problems, arthritis, and rheumatism. This is useful because these are exactly the ailments that afflict the snow goose person. The birch is considered to be the tree of knowledge and ancient forgotten wisdoms; thus, if you were born under this sign, you will ensure that you are a master of your chosen subject.

QUARTZ CRYSTAL

The mineral quartz crystal is associated with the earth-renewal Moon. Quartz is a "power stone" that transmits healing energy. People born under this sign are prone to follow a spiritual path, often by healing and helping others. Being born under this sign is also an indication of psychic abilities.

TRAITS OF PEOPLE BORN UNDER THE SIGN OF THE SNOW GOOSE

If you were born under the sign of the snow goose, you are a practical person who tends to like everything to be in order. You are a serious character with a dry sense of humor. If you were born under the sign of the snow goose, you are independent and as steady as a rock, the kind of person everyone turns to in a crisis. Snow geese reflect earthy qualities. Mostly cautious but quietly confident, you can be obstinate and strong willed. You are very hardworking and you hate to let others down.

Those who are born under the sign of the snow goose are practical managers who set high standards for themselves and others. It can be quite hard to live up to these people's expectations sometimes! People born under the sign of the snow goose are also quite self-critical. They work well in a disciplined environment but demand equal measures from subordinates. Highly organized, they excel in multitasking and juggling more than one project at a time. Although firm, these individuals are also fair to the people they deal with. Those who are born under the sign of the snow goose value tradition.

THE SNOW GOOSE'S POSITIVE TRAITS

People born under the sign of the snow goose are goal oriented. They seek positions where they can have great control and authority, so they do not function well in subordinate positions. If they believe they can succeed in attaining a goal, they will persevere until it is reached. These people tend to be profound thinkers. They consider life to be a serious business, and the need to be in control of it is paramount. They are seekers after knowledge and wisdom. Rational, logical, and clearheaded, they have excellent concentration and delight in all forms of debate.

Extremely loyal and rarely impetuous, people born under this sign consider business and personal relationships carefully before committing. Once they have formed a bond, they do not break it easily. For them, family always comes first. In short, people born under the sign of the snow goose are ambitious, hardworking, responsible, practical, and self-disciplined.

THE SNOW GOOSE'S NEGATIVE TRAITS

Unfortunately, individuals born under the sign of the snow goose are pessimistic by nature, which explains the dry sense of humor, which sometimes comes across as irony or sarcasm. These people can spread doom and gloom in a minute, and they are quite capable of depressing other people. Often downhearted, people born under this sign need a positive environment where everything is in its allotted place. They can be stubborn, overbearing, unforgiving, and condescending.

In personal relationships, people born under the sign of the snow goose tend to be uncomfortable and can be suspicious of others. These individuals have few close friends, and they can be indifferent to those who are outside their circle. For such a supposedly dour sign, one would imagine these people to be silent and withdrawn, but this is not at all the case. Most are chatty and sociable, while some are talking machines that do not allow others to get a word in edgewise.

THE SNOW GOOSE AND PROFESSION

Many born under the sign of the snow goose choose a professional career such as that of doctor, lawyer, or accountant. These people are especially good dealing with money. They excel as bureaucrats, especially when dealing with demanding projects.

Those born under the sign of the snow goose also make excellent politicians due to their skill in debate, and they are often good teachers. They do best in an environment where they can exercise their desire for authority and organization. There are many people of this sign in publishing. Indeed, one department of a large publishing house employed ten people—nine of whom were born under the sign of the snow goose!

People born under this sign are good with their hands so may take up engineering, farming, or building work. Occasionally they will go into the entertainment industry, where their dry wit can be used to make people laugh.

THE SNOW GOOSE AND COMPATIBILITY

Those born under the sign of the snow goose belong to the turtle clan, so they get along well with others of that clan, such as people born under the sign of the beaver or the grizzly bear. They can be reasonably happy in the company of those who belong to the frog clan, such as those born under the sign of the cougar, flicker (a type of woodpecker), or snake.

Famous People Born under the Sign of the Snow Goose

Joan Baez

David Bowie

Nicolas Cage

Jim Carrey

Marlene Dietrich

Jane Fonda

Maurice and Robin Gibb

Mel Gibson

Martin Luther King

Richard Nixon

Elvis Presley

9

THE OTTER
January 20 - February 18

Clan	Butterfly
Spirit keeper	Spirit Keeper of the North
Moon	Rest-and-cleansing Moon
Crystal or mineral	Silver
Tree or plant	Aspen
Color	Silver

THE REST-AND-CLEANSING MOON

During the rest-and-cleansing Moon period, nothing much is happening in the fields and the countryside, so this is the time for the clan to rest, to clean the household, farming areas, and tools, and to clear up the vegetable patch in readiness for the coming spring. There is time now for people to communicate with one another and to get to know new children in the clan or new clan members. In short, this sign represents communication of all kinds.

The rest-and-cleansing Moon teaches you to be a great communicator. You truly like people, yourself included. You excel in communications and romance and have the ability to be clever and bold in life. People born under this time have psychic abilities and are humanitarians, although they do need to avoid being taken in by people who are frauds.

THE OTTER

The charming and friendly otter is the most playful of animals in the wild. Both river and sea otters are happy when entertaining others. Otters are members of the weasel family who depend on the waters of large lakes, rivers, and the sea. Sea otters almost became extinct when people killed them for their fur. All otters have large appetites. The highly intelligent otter is one of the few animals that can utilize tools, for instance, using rocks to open shells. Otters have a wide vocal range consisting of chirps, squeals, screeches, hiccups, chuckles, and hisses, and their calls can carry for a mile. When not eating, hunting, playing, or sunning themselves, otters sleep.

Otters have warm and active homes, and both parents assist in raising their young. Otters are lifelong companions to each other, and a mate will mourn the death of his or her partner. Noble, curious, and playful, the otter is loyal and loving to others.

THE ASPEN

The leaves from the aspen tree can be used to make a tonic or a tea that will help with liver or digestive problems. It can also be used as a relaxant, and for faintness, hay fever, and skin conditions such as eczema. The bark can be used as a deodorant, and a brew made from the bark is said to prevent congestion in the body. The aspen is believed to be a magical tree due to the bell-like song of the silver leaves when they are blowing in the wind.

SILVER

Silver is considered to be one of Earth's most precious minerals. Silver is malleable; it has been shaped into many art forms. It has an emotional energy flow that helps to release negative congestion in life. Silver encourages intuitive, telepathic, and visionary qualities, and wearing it can help to heal the highest levels of consciousness.

TRAITS OF PEOPLE BORN UNDER THE SIGN OF THE OTTER

If you were born under the sign of the otter, you are one of the most interesting and attractive people. You can by shy, sensitive, gentle, and patient, or enthusiastic and lively with a tendency to be an exhibitionist. Both types are very strong willed and forceful in their own way. You can be very opinionated with strong convictions, and you will fight for what you believe in, arguing vehemently for what you believe to be true.

People born under the sign of the otter are farsighted and innovative. They are generally without prejudice and quite tolerant of the points of view of others. These individuals can see a valid argument even when they disagree with it, and being objective, they never get waylaid by being too close to an issue or a person.

Those born under the sign of the otter are humane. Known to be frank and outspoken, they are serious and genial companions. In short, these people are refined, idealistic, and romantic, but also practical. Personable and likable, they are quick in mind and quick to respond. They rarely wear their hearts on their sleeves, but once committed, those born under the sign of the otter are committed for life.

THE OTTER'S POSITIVE TRAITS

People born under the sign of the otter are usually intelligent, cool, clear-sighted, and logical. These people have good imaginations and are quite intuitive. They are drawn to and inspired by great causes. These people are not limited to their environment. Disappointments do not deter them from their goals. People born under the sign of the otter often adopt a lifestyle that goes against the tide, because anything that is unusual and unique fascinates them. These people, both the retiring kind and the outgoing type, like their space and need to spend some time alone. They enjoy their own company and are recharged by this quiet time.

Rarely content to be followers, people born under this sign are often society's trendsetters. They do not take kindly to interference by others, even if it is well intended. Most people born under the sign of the otter appreciate beauty and balance, possessing an excellent sense of aesthetics. Their interests might include drama, music, art, and science. The main positive traits of these individuals are a forward-looking mind, independence, inventiveness, friendliness, a humanitarian outlook, and originality.

THE OTTER'S NEGATIVE TRAITS

Despite the warmth and kindness found in people born under the sign of the otter, they can often be quite aloof. They often do not actively seek out relationships, and they resent infringement on their time and resources. They are engaging yet unreachable at times, and while they can be fascinating and dynamic one moment, they can lack real warmth at another. They are extremely logical when it comes to considering the problems of others, so they cannot understand why other people get so emotional or upset, but when it comes to their own problems, they can become emotional, tense, and very angry.

Among their faults are extreme eccentricity and an unwillingness to participate in conventional behavior or established protocol. They can be jealous, possessive, and demanding. When angered, they become extremely rude. They do not appreciate possessive, jealous, and demanding behavior in others though!

The main negative traits of those born under the sign of the otter are a tendency to withdraw and become unemotional, aloof, temperamental, unpredictable, and weird. These individuals also have very fixed opinions.

THE OTTER AND PROFESSION

Many born under the otter sign work best in group projects, but they must have a leading role. They make excellent researchers and scientists, especially astronomers and historians. They may lead the field in photography, computer technology, and electronics. In the arts and humanities, their progressive talents are expressed well in writing, particularly in poetry and humor, and in broadcasting. Otters make good character actors and they are natural mimics. They also make wonderful musicians.

Many are interested in astrology and similar mind, body, and spirit subjects of a technical nature, and some manage to make a living in these fields.

THE OTTER AND COMPATIBILITY

People born under the otter sign belong to the butterfly clan, so they get along very well with other people in that clan, such as those born under the sign of the deer or the raven. Otherwise, they are reasonably happy with members of the thunderbird clan, such as people born under the sign of the red-tailed hawk, the sturgeon, or the elk.

Famous People Born under the Sign of the Otter

Robbie Burns

Lewis Carroll

Charles Dickens

Christian Dior

Bridget Fonda

Abraham Lincoln

Wolfgang Amadeus Mozart

Paul Newman

Ronald Reagan

Jerry Springer

Oprah Winfrey

10

THE COUGAR
February 19 – March 20

Clan	Frog
Spirit keeper	Spirit Keeper of the North
Moon	Big-winds Moon
Crystal or mineral	Turquoise
Tree or plant	Plantain
Color	Turquoise

THE BIG-WINDS MOON

The sign of the cougar comes under the big-winds Moon, the third Moon on the Native American astrology wheel. Big-winds Moon people can be moody. They are very sensitive and can lose their temper quickly.

The big-winds Moon teaches you to have a great yearning for spirituality, making you psychic and able to create your own medicinal remedies. As the cougar, you are hesitant to express your true feelings at times, and you have a mysterious air about your presence.

THE COUGAR

The cougar is an animal that is feared and misunderstood. The cougar, also known as the mountain lion, the puma, and even the panther, is a member of the feline family; it can weigh from 150 to 300 pounds. Cougars were found all across the United States before civilization. Now they are found mainly in the western United States. The best climbers of all the felines, cougars are also swift runners. They have large individual territories, and they do not allow their territories to overlap. Cougars are hunters, and they like to chase. They often work with their mates or relations to hunt, and they hunt for only what they can eat. They hunt farm livestock only when their natural food supplies have run out. The female cougar is a better hunter than the male.

When cougars mate, the female frequently is the aggressor. Most litters are born in the spring, and the mother cougar is very loving to her kittens. The father cougar does not have much to do with the litter.

When working on a spiritual vibration, cougars can teach you about speed, grace, territoriality, sensitivity, mystery, and communication.

THE PLANTAIN

The leaves of the plantain plant can be used internally as a tea or externally as a compress to cool, soothe, and heal. The plantain is an excellent blood cleanser, which helps alleviate pain. The plantain can be used as a tea, a compress, or as a soak in a bathtub, and it can help heal inflammation. It also helps heal kidney and bladder problems. The plantain is a reminder of the eternal promise of new life. Its deep roots demonstrate stability, to help ground you to the Earth.

The fruit of the plantain is closely related to the common banana and is filled with potassium, which can alleviate depression.

TURQUOISE

Turquoise is considered one of Earth's most protective minerals. Many Native American peoples believe that this mineral will protect them from danger and injury. In the past turquoise was used on shields to ward off enemies.

Turquoise promotes healing and strengthens healing already in process. This stone helps the owner to create natural medicine and helps him or her to understand the mysteries of the universe. Turquoise has calming qualities, so it is a good choice to give someone who is going through a difficult time.

TRAITS OF PEOPLE BORN UNDER THE SIGN OF THE COUGAR

If you were born under the sign of the cougar you are one of the most malleable of the twelve signs. You possess a gentle, patient nature, but one that can be molded. Those born under the cougar sign can be impressed and completely absorbed into their environment, and they adapt to their surroundings quickly, whether good or bad.

People born under the sign of the cougar are generous, friendly, and good-natured, with a sense of kindness and compassion. These people are sensitive to everything around them, including the feelings of others. They are popular folk because of their easy and likable manner. They have an uncanny sense of perceiving what others need, and they can often deliver it. These individuals are not initiators, because they would rather allow circumstances and events to unfold around them and motivate them. When faced with change, they respond quickly and efficiently.

People born under the sign of the cougar are not practical people. They are too ephemeral for normal day-to-day living. They are sensitive and instinctual, rather than intellectual or mechanical. When they find the right route forward, they are capable of some incredible deeds. They might then become completely absorbed in their chosen path or field, to the exclusion of everything else.

THE COUGAR'S POSITIVE TRAITS

Those born under the sign of the cougar are usually gifted artistically and excel when they are in an environment where they can use their imagination and intuition. They are versatile, and they tend to understand things by absorption rather than logic. These loyal individuals love their homes and families and are kind and generous. They are receptive to new ideas and circumstances and can adapt to change easily.

People born under the sign of the cougar can make a success of themselves in any kind of artistic or creative field, because they have great imaginations. They possess wonderful creativity, which is demonstrated in music, literature, drama, and the arts. They appreciate luxury and pleasure, and they are ripe for new sensations. When these individuals travel, they prefer remote, exotic destinations.

Most people born under this sign are understanding, instinctive, compassionate, artistic, self-sacrificing, and charitable.

THE COUGAR'S NEGATIVE TRAITS

Those born under the sign of the cougar are absentminded at times and do not fare well in a controlled or fixed environment. If forced to live in such a situation, they will soon rebel against convention. They take everything personally, and because they are so sensitive and emotional, they can end up being a drain on the resources of others. In business they can be unreliable, idle, careless, and impractical, as they are often fickle and unfaithful. They get bored easily when they feel that they are being controlled. They can also be gullible and can rely on others too much at times.

Often those born under this sign can be misled because they want to believe in others. No matter how often they are led astray by vacant promises, they keep the faith and go on looking for their personal ideal. Their dreamy and impractical natures are a source of distress to those close to them. Being a mixture of optimism and pessimism, these individuals find it hard to make up their minds on any issue.

The worst aspect of those who are born under this sign is their ability to switch from being a sweet-natured soul into a sharp-tongued, spiteful tyrant. They do not trust others to do things properly, so they tend to check up on even simple things, and they may even be malicious enough to spend time watching others in order to catch them doing something wrong.

THE COUGAR AND PROFESSION

In the career department, people born under the cougar sign are better in self-employment than working for someone else, but they are not the best businesspeople, so their ideal situation is to be in charge of their own job, while someone else has the ultimate financial responsibility. Their sympathy equips them for careers in charity, catering to the needy, nursing and looking after the sick and helpless, or veterinary medicine.

Those born under this sign have a love of water and can be found in work that keeps them near the sea. Their creativity includes a natural ability to imitate or mirror other people or to enter into other people's feelings. These attributes make

them wonderful character actors, and many find great fulfill-
ment on stage or in films, or indeed by working behind the
scenes in the entertainment industry.

Individuals born under the sign of the cougar have a kind of
instinct about people that makes them effective in teaching,
local government, or the legal area. Many work in law
enforcement or the judicial system. Their intuitive and spiritual qualities can lead them into careers in religion or as
mediums and mystics, while others make great chefs and
cooks. Because of their versatility and plasticity, they often
follow several vocations during their lifetime.

THE COUGAR AND COMPATIBILITY

Cougars are members of the frog clan, so they are compatible with other members of this clan, such as those born
under the signs of the flicker and the snake. They also get
along well with members of the turtle clan, such as those
born under the sign of the snow goose, the beaver, or the
grizzly bear.

Famous People Born under the Sign of the Cougar

Drew Barrymore

Alexander Graham Bell

Sir Richard Burton

Edgar Cayce

Nat King Cole

Albert Einstein

George Harrison

Edward Kennedy

Jerry Lewis

Rupert Murdoch

John Steinbeck

Elizabeth Taylor

George Washington

Bruce Willis

11

THE RED-TAILED HAWK
March 21 – April 19

Clan	*Thunderbird*
Spirit keeper	*Spirit Keeper of the East*
Moon	*Budding-trees Moon*
Crystal or mineral	*Opal*
Tree or plant	*Dandelion*
Color	*Yellow*

THE BUDDING-TREES MOON

The sign of the red-tailed hawk comes under the budding-trees Moon, the first Moon of the Spirit Keeper of the East. On the Native American astrology wheel, this Moon is found at the spring equinox. People who are connected to the budding-trees Moon can be excellent leaders and are often clear-sighted, although they may need to learn to channel their energies and be more patient with other people.

THE RED-TAILED HAWK

The red-tailed hawk is the only hawk with a broad wingspan and fan-shaped wings. Farmers often call the red-tailed hawk the "chicken hawk," because they insist that it steals their poultry. Crows, magpies, and overprotective songbirds sometimes attack red-tailed hawks during territorial disputes. These attacks rarely end in injury to the red-tailed hawk, so the birds can go on to live to be fourteen years of age. They usually nest in tall trees, and they are found all over the United States, but mainly in the western states. Both parents of the red-tailed hawk look after their young. They are very adaptable birds, and they can survive almost anywhere, as long as the location is one where humans will not disturb them. Their call is like the sound of steam escaping a kettle, and they are magnificent flyers.

Red-tailed hawks are special to Native American peoples. The Pueblo people referred to them as "red eagles." Like the eagle, they have a special connection with the sky and the Sun. Because the hawks fly high, they are thought to have magical powers, and their feathers are often used in ceremonial prayers to the Sun and the wind. Their feathers are also used in healing ceremonies. The red-tailed hawk is often used to refer to the head of a clan because of the great importance and status with which the bird is credited.

If you work on a spiritual vibration, studying the habits of the red-tailed hawk can teach you about grace, flying, survival, clear-sightedness, intensity, optimism, and openness.

THE DANDELION

The dandelion has many uses. The root is often used as a good substitute for coffee, and it is an herbal remedy as well as a cooking herb. The leaves are often used in salads in Western countries. They are high in vitamins A, B, and C and are a good source of iron and natural sodium. The dandelion is soothing, relaxing, and mildly sedating. It can be used to effectively cleanse the organs of the body.

The dandelion also helps to purify and alkalize the bloodstream. It can help to balance all the organs in the body and can remind you of the necessity of exploration and experimentation in the beauty of various stages of growth. This plant has a long history of use as a diuretic, so much so that it is actually called *pissenlit* in French, meaning literally, wet the bed!

OPAL

Fire opal is the mineral associated with the budding-trees Moon. The stone is believed to hold within it the powers of the Sun, Moon, and fire. It sparks energy and teaches about harnessing the life force. The opal can be used to increase mental, physical, and emotional energy, so it is a great mineral to use for lethargy and fatigue. It counteracts stagnation on all levels of life.

On a spiritual vibration, the opal enhances existing physical and emotional qualities and aids one on the journey of life. Opals can assist in understanding others, and they are said to enhance sexuality and power.

TRAITS OF PEOPLE BORN UNDER THE SIGN OF THE RED-TAILED HAWK

People born under the sign of the red-tailed hawk are open, enthusiastic, and individualistic. They can be outspoken, alert, and quick to act and speak, and they would rather speak than listen. These individuals are ambitious, with lots of drive and a strong desire to lead. They make poor followers. They are fiercely independent, and they usually take the side of the underdog in any controversy. People born under this sign are champions of lost causes and battles. This trait is due to a strong belief in their ability to turn any situation around.

Those born under the sign of the red-tailed hawk are more intellectual than spiritual, and they are people of action rather than dreamers. They demonstrate little subtlety, and they are frank and amiable, so they make quick decisions and grasp ideas very quickly. Individuals born under the sign of the red-tailed hawk are also quick to anger; they are known for their impatience, and they can be prone to arrogance.

People born under this sign have a strong self-image and the ability to size up a situation in an instant, to some extent through intuition. These people calculate risks with lightning speed and make decisions accordingly. An adage that fits these individuals well is "A straight line is the shortest distance between two points." They do not waste time and energy beating around the bush; they come straight to the point.

THE RED-TAILED HAWK'S POSITIVE TRAITS

People born under the sign of the red-tailed hawk are known to be very generous. They give their time, money, and effort, and they sympathize with people who are less fortunate than they are. They have both moral and physical courage and will support anyone they believe is being treated unfairly. Red-tailed hawk people are creative and open hearted. These people are high spirited and pioneering, dynamic and independent. They are confident, courageous, and creative and often the leaders in any situation. Their presence in dangerous situations often reassures people and provides proper leadership when it is needed.

People born under this sign love having plenty of every-thing, so their homes are full of books, gadgets, tools, and clothes. Many take on do-it-yourself jobs, rather than hire someone to do the job, which can often lead to jobs being half finished. Some individuals born under this sign are more careful than this; they are true craftspeople who can make or repair absolutely anything. These individuals are good to their children. During their spare time, they love lis-tening to music.

THE RED-TAILED HAWK'S NEGATIVE TRAITS

Individuals born under the sign of the red-tailed hawk have a high-energy output, which can be a cause for anxiety for those who live or work alongside them. Sometimes these individuals' anxiety is so intense and unimaginable that they will abandon a venture out of fear of failure. They will then redirect their energy into something new, which can mean jobs being abandoned when they are half done. Another flaw in people born under the sign of the red-tailed hawk is their fear of rejection—it is on the top of their list of fears. If they are not certain of acceptance, they will reject a plan or even the company of others out of hand before others reject their ideas and their company. They believe that the best defense is a good offense.

Some people born under the sign of the red-tailed hawk are extremely adroit politically. This is a fine trait if they do not lose their idealism, but some are so ambitious that they jettison good friends along the way. At worst, they can be moody, quick-tempered, violent, impatient, and intolerant of others.

THE RED-TAILED HAWK AND PROFESSION

The best career by far for this sign is teaching. People born under the sign of the red-tailed hawk can teach anyone from small children to adults, but they are especially good with school-age children or teenagers. If they do not teach for a living, they should train scouts, cadets, dancers, or some other type of youth group. They can even care for young offenders or other youngsters who have lost their way.

In the career department, these individuals need to take charge; a routine or monotonous job is not meant for them. Their originality, imagination, and great mental and physical energy show that they require work in which they can utilize all these traits. These people prefer to work on their own or to direct others.

Individuals born under this sign can communicate with the public, so a career in journalism, publicity, advertising, publishing, radio, or television is a natural profession for them to be in. The military, with its many leadership possibilities, is another field that is ripe for these individuals. Law enforcement is another vocation that is attractive to those born under this sign. In a similar capacity, these individuals can make excellent surgeons or surgical nurses. In the arts and entertainment field, these people do very well. They are endowed with so many valuable assets that they are rarely in a job they do not like, and they always use their imaginative and intuitive nature to benefit themselves and others.

Gifted artistically and imaginatively, if these individuals become interested in art, they can do very well. Many are excellent dancers, and even those who just bop around on the dance floor for fun are extremely agile and light on their feet. They appreciate luxury and pleasure and are always on the lookout for new and exciting places to visit and see.

THE RED-TAILED HAWK AND COMPATIBILITY

People born under the sign of the red-tailed hawk are members of the thunderbird clan, so they get along well with other members of the thunderbird clan, such as those born under the sign of the sturgeon or the elk. They also get along reasonably well with members of the butterfly clan, such as those born under the sign of the otter, deer, or raven.

Famous People Born under the Sign of the Red-Tailed Hawk

Hans Christian Andersen

Warren Beatty

Jackie Chan

Charlie Chaplin

Joan Crawford

Russell Crow (great name for someone born under the sign of the red-tailed hawk!)

Celine Dion

Vincent van Gogh

Thomas Jefferson

Elton John

Eddie Murphy

Colin Powell

Leonardo da Vinci

William Wordsworth

12

THE BEAVER
April 20 - May 20

Clan	*Turtle*
Spirit keeper	*Spirit Keeper of the East*
Moon	*Frogs-return Moon*
Crystal or mineral	*Chrysocolla*
Tree or plant	*Blue camas*
Color	*Blue*

FROGS–RETURN MOON

People who are connected to the frogs-return Moon value hard work and have a natural ability to create a beautiful environment around them. When working on a spiritual vibration, the frogs-return Moon teaches perseverance, patience, and stability, although these people need to guard against becoming too stubborn and refusing to ask for help.

THE BEAVER

The beaver is the only animal capable of changing its environment in order to create its own peace, security, and contentment. Adult beavers weigh between thirty and seventy pounds and can grow up to three or four feet in length. Beavers do not make many sounds. Occasionally they bark, hiss, or mew in the privacy of their lodges. To warn of danger, beavers slap their long, rudderlike tails on the ground. Beavers mate for life and are affectionate parents who stay around their young for around two years, or until the next litter comes.

Beavers are land mammals that spend a lot of time in the water, and their bodies are amazingly engineered to their habitat. Indeed, their adaptable bodies could have made them one of the most dominant animals on earth if it was not for humans. It is unfortunate that human beings found a use for beaver fur in the manufacture of men's hats. Beavers have also been hunted for a special gland that produces castoreum, a supposed cure-all from the time of the early Greeks until the eighteenth century. One way or another, beavers were in such demand that, by the 1800s, they were almost driven to extinction. Finally, humans discovered that beavers actually helped the environment with their dam building and were of great value to fishing, wildlife, vegetation, and aesthetics, and this usefulness saved them.

Native Americans valued the beaver's fur and meat and used the castoreum to effect healing. When the Europeans arrived in North America, they encouraged the Native Americans to hunt more beavers so that they could trade goods for the beaver fur.

Working on a spiritual vibration with the beaver can teach you about stability, balance, tradition, and the true value of things. The beaver also shows us how to be affectionate, hardworking, and self-reliant.

THE BLUE CAMAS

The blue camas was an important food source for Native Americans. It was essential that they used only the camas that had blue flowers, as plants with yellow or greenish white flowers are poisonous. Blue camas is a good food staple and can be used to make pancakes and molasses and can serve as a sugar substitute. Blue camas is said to be good for balancing the blood sugar levels in the body, and the plant is excellent for creating movement where there is stagnation.

CHRYSOCOLLA

The chrysocolla is the mineral associated with the frogs-return Moon; it represents the elements of the earth and sky within you. It assists you in reaching your goals and keeping a firm foundation on the Earth. The chrysocolla teaches people to learn to balance the earth and the sky within themselves.

Chrysocolla is a stone of good medicine that can bring you good luck and good health. It is said to purify the heart, mind, and spirit. This mineral is ideal for anyone who needs grounding, as it promotes a feeling of peace, giving the wearer a stronger connection with Earth.

TRAITS OF PEOPLE BORN UNDER THE SIGN OF THE BEAVER

People born under the sign of the beaver tend to be slow, methodical, practical, and reserved. They are also stolid, tenacious, and determined, possessing tremendous willpower and self-discipline. These people are inclined to stick to tried and tested methods of thinking, and their greatest satisfaction derives from results produced directly by their own personal efforts, rather than by those of others.

Roots are very important to the people born under this sign, and they need a sense of permanence and security. They are usually very easygoing and slow to anger, but once roused, they can have a fierce temper; they can be very difficult to deal with when they get angry. Loyalty is very important to these individuals, and a true friend will speak well of their great generosity. Honesty, integrity, and dependability are noticeable characteristics of people born under this sign. They are extremely sensible where money is concerned.

These people have what baseball players would call the "safest hands" in the zodiac. This means that they literally do not drop anything—be it fly balls, plates, or tools. People born under the sign of the beaver can work as well with their hands as beavers themselves work with their paws, and virtually all people born under the beaver sign could erect a dam and catch fish in it with great efficiency if they put their minds to it.

THE BEAVER'S POSITIVE TRAITS

People born under the sign of the beaver are very warm and loving, gentle, and charming—most of the time. They are self-motivated, and once they set their sights on something, they generally get it. These individuals weigh the pros and cons of every situation and are careful not to make rash decisions. To more impulsive people, these individuals appear to be boring, but once people born under this sign make a decision, they are usually proved to be right. People born under this sign can be relied upon to turn up at work every day and to do what needs to be done. They hate to be rushed, so they work best at jobs that do not need to be done in a great hurry. They are extremely good with people, as they do not take offense or get unduly ruffled without good reason.

People born under the beaver sign are usually physical people who make an effort to keep fit and healthy, although they have to watch their food intake because they can get fat if they are not careful. They love the Earth and they enjoy obtaining and looking after material possessions. They love to treat those around them very well. They are stable, dependable, practical, conventional, determined, and patient.

Many of these individuals have a creative or artistic side to them, with a love of music, gardening, and singing at the top of their lists. Some are wonderfully creative cooks.

THE BEAVER'S NEGATIVE TRAITS

Individuals born under the sign of the beaver can be extremely jealous, possessive, and very stubborn, and they find it extremely hard to adapt to changing circumstances. Some are far too materialistic, which can lead them to become stingy hoarders. They must strive to keep open minds, because their strong personal convictions can blind them to the ideas of others. They take risks only if absolutely necessary, and only after much consideration. People born under this sign are slow to change; they prefer a steady routine in life. Seeming to defy their reputation for hard work and common sense, some are intensely lazy and apt to leave money worries to their partners.

THE BEAVER AND PROFESSION

Clever at developing wealth and maintaining it, these individuals do well in banking and finance. In business they shine in fields concerned with the earth and money. Suitable professions for these people include architect, builder, gardener, accountant, financier, banker, real-estate broker, or anything in the business world. They often possess good singing voices and find real pleasure in singing. Gifted with a natural artistic nature, they make excellent craft workers.

Persistence and single-mindedness are the qualities and trademarks of this sign, so no details are ever overlooked. People born under this sign can be slow and lazy, but many are very dedicated and hardworking.

THE BEAVER AND COMPATIBILITY

Individuals born under the sign of the beaver are members of the turtle clan, so they get along well with other clan members, such as those born under the sign of the snow goose or the grizzly bear. They are also relatively compatible with members of the frog clan, such as people born under the sign of the cougar, flicker, or snake.

Famous People Born under the Sign of the Beaver

Andre Agassi	Joe Lewis
Tony Blair	Karl Marx
Charlotte Bronte	Evita Peron
Pierce Brosnan	William Shakespeare
George Clooney	Barbara Streisand
Bing Crosby	Harry Truman
Queen Elizabeth II	Rudolph Valentino
Sigmund Freud	John Wayne

13

THE DEER
May 21 - June 20

Clan	*Turtle*
Spirit keeper	*Spirit Keeper of the East*
Moon	*Corn-planting Moon*
Crystal or mineral	*Moss agate*
Tree or plant	*Yarrow*
Color	*Pale green*

THE CORN-PLANTING MOON

Corn is not the same thing in other parts of the world as it is in America. The corn that the Native Americans would be planting at this late stage of the year is maize, which is also known as sweet corn in the form that we buy in supermarkets. Throughout Africa, these maize plants are called mealies. When Europeans talk about corn, they usually mean wheat, but they might also be referring to oats, rye, or any other form of cereal.

Corn, by any of its names, is a staple carbohydrate of the kind that forms the background to the human diet anywhere in the world, whatever it happens to be (e.g., rice, potato, etc.). Planting and tending the major staple carbohydrate is an important matter for all societies, and it takes planning, effort, and concentration. These are all concepts that are relatively alien to the deer personality, so the message here is that one must focus, concentrate, put one's shoulder to the wheel, and work for a living!

THE DEER

The deer is one of the most graceful and alert creatures of all. Their beauty brings joy to all that see them. Deer range between two and four feet at the shoulder. They have a bleating but quiet voice and will snort when excited. Deer squeal when they feel under threat of attack, and they also have a special bleat to call their fawns. Fawns are born with a spotted coat, which acts as camouflage.

Deer follow certain practices during each season. Bucks (male deer) have antlers for their protection and for use during the mating season, when they will use them to chase away potential rivals or to keep other deer away from their mates. Deer live in herds or small groups with others of their own sex, except during the mating season. After mating, an older doe usually leads the way to a safe place for the other does to give birth. Many give birth to twins and even triplets. The main killers of deer are dogs, bears, bobcats, forest fires, humans, and automobiles.

Deer played a very important part in the circle of life for many Native American peoples. They provided a staple food, and Native Americans would honor the deer's gift with ceremonies, dances, and prayers. To some tribes, notably the Huichol in Mexico, the deer was the most important of animals. It was seen to represent the heart, and it was called "the gatekeeper to the spirit world." The deer dance is the most sacred dance to Native Americans; they believe that it helps them to pierce the veil between the two worlds.

Working spiritually with the deer can teach you about adaptability, camouflage, grace, beauty, speed, and healing, and this process will also give you connection with the world of spirit.

YARROW

Yarrow is a terrific tonic and strengthener. It has been used with good results as a blood cleanser. Yarrow is an herb that helps conquer the flu virus and is excellent at stopping bleeding. Externally, yarrow acts as a local anesthetic and disinfectant and can also help relieve toothache. Yarrow is also an aid to the lungs, glands, and bronchial tubes, and it will give the user inner strength. Yarrow relates to healing and seeing one's own inner beauty and the beauty within others.

MOSS AGATE

Moss agate brings balance to all parts of the body and has been used in rainmaking ceremonies. It is believed to be the stone that bridges the gap between the animal and the human kingdoms. It can help those who are suffering from emotional problems, and it will alleviate depression and help to ground and energize you.

On a spiritual vibration, moss agate teaches people to clearly see their link with the mineral and plant kingdom.

TRAITS OF PEOPLE BORN UNDER THE SIGN OF THE DEER

People born under the sign of the deer interact with the environment, and investigate, learn, and share ideas. Those born under this intellectual sign value all mental activity, words, and ideas. Communication is of great importance to these individuals, and knowledge is never a thing to be hoarded. Rarely will you find these people more entertained than when they are in the midst of exchanging ideas with others of a similar intellectual nature.

Born under the sign of the most versatile of the medicine wheel animals, these individuals are seldom what they seem. Almost chameleonlike, they will take a stand, voice an opinion, and then change it the following day. Nothing is ever set in stone with them. They are true free spirits who are driven by curiosity. People born under the deer sign will usually have several projects going on at any one time—they can thrive on chaos.

Bright, witty, and entertaining, people born under the sign of the deer are rarely deeply absorbed by any one task. They prefer to skim the surface of many things than to get deeply involved in any one particular interest. Even if they become drawn into something, they will always feel that they are missing out on something else.

THE DEER'S POSITIVE TRAITS

People born under the sign of the deer, one of the most optimistic of all the signs, look forward to each new day. They possess great enthusiasm, and routine is boring for them. Due to their active imagination, they can appear restless. They live by the motto that life must be lived to the fullest. Despite their habit of jumping from one idea to the next, they tend to focus on the two most important things in life—their jobs and their main relationships. Individuals born under this sign must work in a field that keeps them in contact with many people and that offers plenty of variety during each day, and as long as they have that and also enjoy their work, they will stay in the job for many years.

These individuals may not be the most faithful people in matters of love, as they seem to need to experiment with a variety of different kinds of lover. However, once they settle down with the right partners, they are fine. Their childlike nature ensures that they always get along with the younger members of their families.

People born under the deer sign analyze everything, sometimes to the point of craziness. Sexy, affectionate, courteous, and kind, they are also generous and thoughtful. They are very expressive and are often gifted with their hands; it seems whatever they touch turns to gold. Their love of communication may also express itself as a love of languages. They have the knack of making life a little more interesting for the rest of the medicine wheel zodiac.

THE DEER'S NEGATIVE TRAITS

People born under the sign of the deer can be up one minute and then suddenly become moody, aggressive, and cynical. This is part of the double-sided nature of everyone born under the sign of the deer. With a low boredom threshold, they need something new going on all the time to keep them interested; it can be hard to keep their attention for long. These individuals can be very fickle, although this is not intentional, because it is their basic nature to be so. Young people born under this sign find it hard to concentrate, so they can be mistakenly thought of as difficult.

The most negative trait of people born under this sign is a tendency to moan and complain about everything. Some truly see the glass not so much half full as not there at all!

THE DEER AND PROFESSION

People born under the sign of the deer need constant change in their working life, and they need to work with a variety of different people. They often opt for a job in which they meet new people on a daily basis, and although some are happy to stay in one place, they do so only if they have a variety of different tasks and a constant change of scenery.

Many people born under this sign choose to work in some form of business, often working for large organizations. Clerical work, telephone work, and public relations are favorite occupations of these individuals. Many find that because of their natural affinity with figures, they fall easily into jobs within the banking industry or accounting. Other natural occupations for people born under this sign are teaching, broadcasting, and journalism or writing of all kinds, especially magazine articles or chapter contributions to books.

People born under this sign are attuned to young people more so than older ones, so they enjoy working with young people and can be very successful at helping youngsters who are unhappy. Some are drawn to the world of psychology or counseling, where they can help a variety of people. Many are fascinated by the theater and film, and go on to become wonderful actors, while the agility of this sign means that many become excellent athletes.

THE DEER AND COMPATIBILITY

Individuals born under the sign of the deer belong to the butterfly clan, so they are compatible with other people in the butterfly clan, such as those born under the sign of the otter or the raven. They also get along well with members of the thunderbird clan, such as those born under the sign of the red-tailed hawk, the sturgeon, or the elk.

Famous People Born under the Sign of the Deer

Helena Bonham Carter	Angelina Jolie
Joan Collins	Tom Jones
Tony Curtis	John F. Kennedy
Sir Arthur Conan Doyle	Nicole Kidman
Bob Dylan	Henry Kissinger
Clint Eastwood	Anna Kournikova
Sir Douglas Fairbanks	Sir Ian McKellen
Ian Fleming	Marilyn Monroe
Judy Garland	Dorothy Sayers
Steffi Graf	Queen Victoria
Bob Hope	Richard Wagner

14

THE FLICKER
June 21 - July 22

Clan	Frog
Spirit keeper	Spirit Keeper of the South
Moon	Strong-Sun Moon
Crystal or mineral	Carnelian
Tree or plant	Wild rose
Color	Pink

THE STRONG—SUN MOON

In the northern hemisphere, the summer solstice comes around June 21. The days are long and the Sun is hot; soon the land and sea will heat up, and the weather will become unbearably hot during the day in some areas. While there is much work to be done, it is worth considering a siesta during the hottest part of the day if you happen to be a farmer or hunter. This is a time to work, rest, and if one is lucky, also play a little.

THE FLICKER

The flicker is a beautifully colored bird. There are two kinds of flicker in the United States: the yellow-shafted flicker, found in the east, and the red-shafted flicker, found west of the Great Plains. Both types can be seen on farms and even in the suburbs. Flickers are drummers who play their songs on wood. Usually they drum on trees, but they can also drum on wooden houses, sometimes to extract insects, but sometimes just for the sheer joy of it. The flicker displays a magnificent talent for music!

The flicker will dig a gourd-shaped hole in a tree trunk for its nest, and flickers make good, caring parents. They nurture their young until they can fend for themselves. The flicker is a special bird to many Native American peoples. Some say the red-shafted flicker has magical powers, because legend says that while it was trying to put out a fire that had been set by the earthquake spirit, it flew too close to the fire. The flames are said to have caught the flicker's wings and tail, hence the red tips on both. Native Americans particularly value flickers because they drum so well. The red flicker feathers are often presented to war spirits and they are often stuck on prayer sticks to ward off spiritual enemies.

Working spiritually with the flicker can teach you about communicating, music, joy, nurturing, courage, protection, and your connection with the universe.

THE WILD ROSE

Beside many other gifts, the fruit of the rose—rose hips—is very high in vitamin C, and rose hip tea is super for curing sore throats, colds, and flu. Rose petal tea can act as a mild astringent and tonic. Rose water is used as an eye lotion and can combat hay fever. The wild rose can refresh the spirit and aid with problems that require a gentle, cooling tonic.

CARNELIAN AGATE

Carnelian agate represents matters of the heart and love. It is good for sustaining a healthy heart. It is said that you can suspend a carnelian on a string and use it to purify the body, to ease bleeding, and to start a healing process within the body. Carrying a carnelian will help you to keep a healthy and open mind and protect you from anyone trying to read your mind. It will also promote health and healing around you. Some traditions say that carrying a carnelian in your purse, wallet, pocketbook, or pocket will help you to prosper.

TRAITS OF PEOPLE BORN UNDER THE SIGN OF THE FLICKER

Individuals born under the sign of the flicker, one of the most perplexing signs, can range from timid, shy, dull, and withdrawn to brilliant, friendly, and famous. They can have a wide range of emotions, and they possess strong parental instincts. Fundamentally, people born under this sign are conservative and home loving by nature. They appreciate the security of a home base to which to retire when the stresses of life become too much to bear.

Individuals born under the sign of the flicker can appear uncompromising and obstinate, but this stance is often a facade that they use to hide insecurity. Their loved ones may see a different character, one with sympathy and sensitivity to others. In their personal relationships, these people are often a mixture of toughness and tenderness. They can be emotional, romantic, and loyal, on one side, and possessive and moody, on the other. When it comes to their loved ones, especially small children and pets, nobody can be more caring.

Those born under the flicker sign can have closed minds, they can be opinionated, and they never forget an injury. They will also never allow others to forget an error. They are led by their emotions, and they will either be the best or the worst of friends. The overall nature of these individuals is deeply emotional. Although reserved, they possess sensitivity and sympathy. Rarely will they stand on pretence. What appears to be out in front is nothing more than a protective shell, but within its tough armor often resides an intuitive and needy individual who yearns for a deep exchange of love and understanding.

THE FLICKER'S POSITIVE TRAITS

People born under the sign of the flicker are strongly influenced by childhood memories and have a tendency to live in the past. They are purposeful, energetic, shrewd, and intuitive. They can be very wise, and they have a philosophical view on life. Some are overimaginative and prone to being victims of fantasy. They have a flair for the dramatic and often possess a talent for art or literature. They tend to absorb their environment, and they can cope with almost any circumstances. They have a natural talent for mimicry. These individuals are protective, nurturing, traditional, understanding, and caring.

THE FLICKER'S NEGATIVE TRAITS

People born under the sign of the flicker can be sulky, devious, angry, moody, and inclined to self-pity at times. They respond foremost to the urges and dictates of their own feelings. The contradictions in their nature may make them feel up one minute and really down the next, but they blame everyone else for the way they feel. By nature these individuals are very giving and selfless, and they should try to avoid falling into the role of martyrs in certain situations just to make others feel happy.

The worst type of person born under this sign can be disloyal, treacherous, selfish, and unreliable. Negative people born under the flicker sign are so into their own needs and feelings that they are able to tune out the needs and feelings of others.

THE FLICKER AND PROFESSION

People born under the sign of the flicker can fit into a wide range of careers. Always interested in what people are thinking, they have an intuitive sense that makes them good investigative journalists, writers, or politicians. They do well in the public sector and may serve in any capacity, from the welfare department to nursing, catering, or politics.

People born under this sign love good living and comfort, and many excel as chefs and housekeepers. They also have a flair for trade or business and are superior organizers, so they often succeed in industry. Some do well in teaching, while others make excellent salespeople. They are certainly persuasive enough to sell anything to anyone when they put their minds to it.

These individuals' love of the past makes them great history buffs or antique collectors. Other suitable vocations are real estate, gardening, and caretaking. They will also excel in anything to do with water, so careers such as a marine biologist might suit them.

COMPATIBILITY AND THE FLICKER

As a member of the frog clan, people born under the flicker sign get along well with other members of the frog clan, such as those born under the sign of the cougar or the snake. They are also happy with members of the turtle clan, which includes people born under the sign of the snow goose, beaver, or grizzly bear.

Famous People Born under the Sign of the Flicker

Georgio Armani	Henry VIII
Julius Caesar	Helen Keller
Bill Cosby	Nelson Mandela
Tom Cruise	George Orwell
Diana, Princess of Wales	Jean Jacques Rousseau
Harrison Ford	Sylvester Stallone
Tom Hanks	Prince William
Ernest Hemingway	Duke of Windsor

15

THE STURGEON
July 23 - August 22

Clan	Thunderbird
Spirit keeper	Spirit Keeper of the South
Moon	Ripe-berries Moon
Crystal or mineral	Garnet and iron
Tree or plant	Raspberry
Color	Red

RIPE-BERRIES MOON

The time of the ripe-berries Moon is a time of plenty when crops are beginning to come in, fruit is ripening, and animals are in good supply, so the clan is eating well and enjoying the seasonal summer fruits and vegetables. This is a time to be happy and to make the most of life.

THE STURGEON

The sturgeon is considered to be the king of the fishes. It is a primitive fish that probably existed on earth long before the dinosaurs disappeared, so it has a long history. The sturgeon comes in a variety of sizes. Sturgeons found in the Great Lakes area were considered the royalty of fishes among Native American peoples. The Ojibwa people believe that the sturgeon represents depth and strength.

Europeans who came to North America did not have the same respect for the sturgeon; they considered it a nuisance when it got caught in their nets. Worldwide demand for its valuable eggs (caviar) has caused the sturgeon to be fished almost to extinction.

Working on a spiritual level with the sturgeon can teach you about determination, perseverance, depth, and knowledge.

This sign actually links to two different kinds of fish, according to which Native American tradition one follows. The other fish is the salmon. This is another truly royal member of the fish family, as it is valued as a food item by just about everybody. Now, of course, salmon are farmed, but in the past, it took real skill to hunt and catch the salmon, even more so when one realizes that fishermen were frequently in competition with the grizzly bear for these prize fish. This fish is also associated with perseverance, as shown by its determination to swim upstream in order to spawn.

THE RASPBERRY

The raspberry has many medicinal properties. The berries are used to cleanse the system of impurities. They can aid in breaking up and expelling gallstones, and they can stimulate the action of the urinary tact. The root is an astringent that heals sore throats. Raspberry tea acts as a compress for wounds and cuts, and it slows bleeding. A tea from the leaves can be used to ease menstrual problems and the pain of childbirth. Raspberry tea acts as a cure-all tonic. A tea made from the twigs of the raspberry is good for colds, flu, and difficulty in breathing.

Spiritual work with the raspberry plant can teach you to find the sweetness among the thorns of life.

GARNET AND IRON

Unusually, this sign has two inorganic items associated with it: garnet and iron. Both are connected to the heart and to blood, and it is said that these minerals can also stimulate the emotions. Garnet can give courage and heart to those who carry it, and it sharpens the instincts so that people who carry it can be aware of danger. If one is in love with someone uncaring, slipping a garnet in the other person's pocket or bag might make the object of one's affections a little more caring.

Iron is good for the blood and the heart, so much so that women rarely suffered from anemia in the days when cooking pots were made of this metal. Iron can remind you of the need to value your experiences. It can encourage a person to be tougher where toughness is needed and to be able to see where that might be the case. Iron can promote the highest good for all concerned.

TRAITS OF PEOPLE BORN UNDER THE SIGN OF THE STURGEON

Individuals born under the sign of the sturgeon, considered to be one of the strongest signs in Native American astrology, are dominant, spontaneous, creative, and extroverted. These people were born to lead. If people born under this sign are ever part of a team-building exercise, just watch what happens. The idea of buckling down and being part of a team is alien to these individuals, so while they may pretend to be interested in the concept, sooner or later (usually sooner) they will put their foot down and take charge. At this point, they will relax and become happy, while everyone falls in behind them in an equally relaxed and happy manner. Now the team will happily achieve any task that you can dream up for them.

People born under the sign of the sturgeon possess grace and dignity, and they have an expansive personality. Ambitious and strong willed, they are positive and confident in their abilities. These people know what they want in life, and they get it. They are not easily daunted, so they persist through the most formidable of circumstances.

Individuals born under this sign can be stubborn; they often refuse to listen to another person's opinions. Because of their positive nature, they will expect the best, and when things do not turn out as they anticipated, they react immediately and badly. If things go against them, their confidence can evaporate, and they can become extremely downhearted. At this time they need a loved one or trusted friend to keep reminding them that they are valuable and that their opinions and actions are not wrong. Fortunately, their bouts of depression dissipate fairly quickly and these individuals soon recover their usual cheerful and demonstrative nature.

THE STURGEON'S POSITIVE TRAITS

People born under the sign of the sturgeon possess a positive nature and do not shrink from adverse circumstances. They like to live on a grand scale and they hate having to put up with anything less than first class. Fortunately, they are hard workers and high earners, so they do not expect others to provide for them. Outgoing, happy, kind, and generous, they are self-expressive and intelligent. Their main positive traits are directness, willpower, generosity, loyalty, high standards, and ambition. If they see an opportunity, they go after it, but not at the expense of other people. These sincere people have a conscience and a powerful inner sense of morality.

THE STURGEON'S NEGATIVE TRAITS

People born under this sign tend to be honest and decent, which can be a weakness because they believe others to be as decent and capable as they are. They can be too gullible, generous, and trusting for their own good. They are not good judges of character and are inclined to set those they like on pedestals and consider them incapable of doing any wrong. Nobody can live up to their expectations, so they are often let down or disappointed. But, they recover quickly.

They are faithful when in love, but while they are still fancy-free, they enjoy many love affairs. They love pleasure and beauty, and this trait quickly drives them into the arms of attractive people. Their own sunny personalities and attractiveness mean that they never have to work hard to find lovers.

They can be deeply hurt by malice or hostility, and they are too sensitive to personal criticism. When their dominance is threatened they can lose their tempers.

THE STURGEON AND PROFESSION

Individuals born under the sign of the sturgeon do well in any career where there is room at the top. In the political arena they keep going until they reach a powerful position—although they are not usually crafty enough to make a career out of politics. A much more likely arena for them is the world of commerce and business, which is why you often find them as president or chairman of large business organizations. They are excellent organizers, managers, and leaders.

Many people born under this sign go into business for themselves. They are naturally ambitious and they prefer to take charge than to follow. They often become big stars of stage or screen, but whatever they choose to do, they make sure they steal the limelight from everyone around them.

Oddly enough, for such a grand-scale personality, these individuals have organized minds, so they happily cope with computers and numbers, all of which enhance their ability to advance in the modern business arena.

COMPATIBILITY AND THE STURGEON

People born under the sign of the sturgeon belong to the thunderbird clan, so they are compatible with other members of the thunderbird clan, such as those born under the sign of the red-tailed hawk or the elk. They also get along well with members of the butterfly clan, such as those born under the sign of the otter, deer, or raven.

Famous People Born under the Sign of the Sturgeon

Neil Armstrong

Napoleon Bonaparte

Madonna Ciccone

Bill Clinton

Deng Xiaoping

Henry Ford

Alfred Hitchcock

Dustin Hoffman

Jennifer Lopez

Jacqueline Onassis

Beatrix Potter

Robert Redford

Arnold Schwarzenegger

Bernard Shaw

Orville Wright

16

THE GRIZZLY BEAR
August 23 - September 22

Clan	Turtle
Spirit keeper	Spirit Keeper of the South
Moon	Harvest Moon
Crystal or mineral	Amethyst
Tree or plant	Violet
Color	Purple

THE HARVEST MOON

Not surprisingly, the time of the harvest moon is a time when the harvest is gathered in and food of all kinds is preserved, packed away, and stored against the coming winter season.

THE GRIZZLY BEAR

The grizzly bear is considered a gentle and yet powerful animal. Grizzly bears make their dens in holes, in caves, beneath buildings, or beneath waterfalls. They are generally careful and quiet, and they eat anything they can get their paws on. Once they reach adulthood, their only enemies are humans and the only dangers they face are forest fires. Bears are naturally curious, and they move slowly, taking in everything around them. They take time to watch and learn from the things they see around them. During their time of hibernation, the females have to be awake to nurse their young, but the males usually continue to sleep.

For the most part, bears have a good and cheerful nature. They are surprisingly clever and adept, so they share many features with humans. They can stand on two legs and most of them can climb trees. They can remove honey from bee-hives. Bears can spear fish with their claws.

To Native American peoples, the bear is a very special animal. Many legends of the animal world recognize them as the spirit keepers and the head of the animal council. In most tribes the bear represents medicine, leadership, and defense of the clan. If you carry out spiritual work with the bear, you can learn about deliberation, pleasure, observation, slow and steady movement, strength, healing, and teaching.

THE VIOLET

The violet symbolizes reserved sentimentality, and it is a powerful medicinal plant that is rich in vitamin C. The violet is good for dissolving toxins in the blood. This plant can assist in healing cancer or ailments in the bowels, and it relieves sore throats, earaches, and headaches. Violet is also good for easing toothaches and high temperatures. In cooking, it can be used as a thickener in stews, salads, jams, and syrups, or it can be dipped in sugar and eaten with chocolate.

Being around violet awakens the heart and helps you understand the depths of your love.

AMETHYST

The amethyst is the mineral associated with the grizzly bear and the harvest Moon. The amethyst is seen as a symbol of courage, justice, and judgment. It is a stone that soothes and pacifies, and it is said to protect against black witchcraft and also against lightning. It helps you achieve spiritual attunement as well as acting as a good balance for physical and spiritual levels.

The amethyst can help you understand the source of your anger and thus help soothe it; it can clarify you when in a dream state. Amethyst is associated with purity within those who carry or wear it.

TRAITS OF PEOPLE BORN UNDER THE SIGN OF THE GRIZZLY BEAR

Individuals born under the sign of the grizzly bear are naturally fastidious regarding cleanliness, hygiene, and health. In this respect, as in all others, they strive for perfection. People born under this sign have attractive personalities and are often witty and charming. Others regard them as efficient, shrewd, and logical. Nevertheless, those born under this sign often feel as though they are not good enough. Some of these feelings may be a holdover from a childhood during which others in the family were valued more highly or where these individuals were made to feel worthless.

People born under the grizzly bear sign seldom seek the spotlight; they are somewhat introverted, and they usually prefer to work behind the scenes. This is actually a strength rather than a weakness, because these painstaking types are just as valuable as the "stars" of this world.

Typical people born under this sign are always immaculate and carry themselves well, projecting an aura of dignity and self-assurance. They are always well groomed and stylish. Natural-born analysts, they strive for perfection in every area of their lives. They find it hard to handle criticism, probably because they are already far too hard on themselves.

THE GRIZZLY BEAR'S POSITIVE TRAITS

People born under the sign of the grizzly bear are efficient, reliable, and hardworking. They are considerate toward others, but their dutiful nature means that others frequently take advantage of them. They have an uncanny knack for choosing partners who are takers rather than givers and who cast them in the role of caring person or provider, especially when they reach their own old age.

Industrious, efficient, and intelligent people, they do not take kindly to being told what to do, even by well-meaning friends. They are independent thinkers who like to work things out for themselves. In their own quiet way, they can be extremely obstinate. They are a very modest bunch of people who will work hard to get to where they want to be. These shy people are wonderful problem solvers.

THE GRIZZLY BEAR'S NEGATIVE TRAITS

Some people born under the sign of the grizzly bear are obsessive about cleanliness, so they can come across to others as being fussy and irritable. They can be nervous about trying new things, and they can be cynical about things they have not yet come across. They need time to adjust to new circumstances, and they like to take things very slowly and weigh up each and every option before making a decision. However, when these individuals have made that decision, they stick to it firmly.

These people can be highly critical toward others, and they can develop a sharp tongue. They see others' failings clearly and can make hurtful remarks. Though they do their duty by their parents and relatives, they can become very tired of their demands. When this happens, they still go through the motions of caring for them, while secretly despising them.

THE GRIZZLY BEAR AND PROFESSION

Those born under the sign of the grizzly bear do well in any career in which they can apply their methodical minds. Many will go into the caring professions, especially in the medical field, as doctors, nurses, hospital administrators, and so on. Others will follow their natural curiosity for science and statistics and go into a career such as a forensic expert, a statistician, a computer analyst, or an engineer. Very common positions for these individuals are bookkeeper, accountant, banker, financial director, statistician, financial analyst, and other number-crunching jobs.

Many people born under this sign make good writers because they can think things out in a slow and structured way. The world of publishing is full of them, especially on the editing side. Many also take up astrology. Any area of work that requires organized thinking patterns suits these people.

COMPATIBILITY AND THE GRIZZLY BEAR

Those born under the sign of the grizzly bear are members of the turtle clan, so they are compatible with those born under the sign of the other two turtle clan members, the snow goose and the beaver. They also get along well with members of the frog clan, such as those born under the sign of the cougar, flicker, or snake.

Famous People Born under the Sign of the Grizzly Bear

Johann Sebastian Bach
Ingrid Bergman
Agatha Christie
Sean Connery
Jimmy Connors
Queen Elizabeth I
Gloria Estefan
Barry Gibb
Greta Garbo
Richard Gere
Prince Harry

Michael Jackson
Stephen King
Tommy Lee Jones
Sophia Loren
Aristotle Onassis
Keanu Reeves
Oliver Stone
Mother Teresa
H.G. Wells
Mary Wollstonecraft
 Shelley

17

THE RAVEN
September 23 - October 23

Clan	Butterfly
Spirit keeper	Spirit Keeper of the West
Moon	Ducks-fly Moon
Crystal or mineral	Jasper
Tree or plant	Mullein
Color	Brown

DUCKS-FLY MOON

The ducks-fly Moon marks the time of the autumn equinox position on the Native American astrology wheel. The message of this sign is that one has to experience discomfort sometimes in order to move on. This sign also encourages people to show physical affection and to be comfortable both on Earth and with their spiritual side.

THE RAVEN

The raven is a black bird with a wedge-shaped tail. Although ravens are found all over the world, they are most often found in the West. Their song is a loud croak, and they can sometimes become quite aggressive, although they are wary of others. Their diet consists of insects, and some eat snails and shellfish, which they drop from the air in order to break the shell. They are very group oriented and very defensive of their territory. The raven holds tribal councils.

To Native American peoples, ravens are considered birds of balance between man and nature. Almost all tribes have stories and legends relating to the raven, usually explaining why it is black. In all of these legends, the raven begins as a white bird whose color is then changed. Sometimes this is said to be a punishment for wrongdoing, but other legends say it is a mark of respect for the danger the bird undertook in an effort to help humans. There is a duality in the way that Native American peoples view these birds. To some the raven is a bad omen, but to others it is a sign of good luck. Ravens have been credited with both bringing dark clouds and holding them away.

Here is a true story about ravens, and it comes not from the mountains and deserts of America but from the soft, green woodlands of southern England. A friend of mine once read about a legend that said that ravens and crows desert an area if they feel that it is going to disappear. One year my friend noticed that the trees and roofs in her suburban area were filling up with ravens, and she remarked to her husband that the heavily wooded countryside of Surrey and Sussex was about to disappear. Her husband had no time for such legends and told my friend that she was talking nonsense. A few weeks later, southern England was struck by a hurricane, and the two counties lost many of their trees and all the usual nesting places and haunts of the ravens along with them. The clever ravens survived, and soon they moved back into the countryside.

THE MULLEIN

The mullein is the plant associated with the raven and the ducks-fly Moon. It is a tall plant and a versatile healer. Tea made from mullein is good for soothing the mucous membranes and is also known to cure the lungs, bladder, heart, kidney, and liver. Mullein helps to alleviate nervous conditions. Used externally, the tea helps to heal hemorrhoids, ulcers, tumors, swelling, and tenderness. Oil made from mullein flowers has long been used for ear infections, warts, bruises, and sprains. Spiritually speaking, mullein can teach you to explore the healing parts of your nature.

JASPER

Jasper brings many blessings. It is a grounding force that can help a person to harmonize with the Earth's energy. It is said that jasper can make its owner invisible, and it can remove poison from snakebite. It is also said to restore eyesight and to bring rain when used in a rain ceremony. Jasper is believed by Native American peoples to give the carrier power over bad spirits, and it both stimulates and brings balance to the owner. Less romantically, perhaps, it is said that if one applies jasper to a wound, it will stop the bleeding.

TRAITS OF PEOPLE BORN UNDER THE SIGN OF THE RAVEN

Those who are born under the sign of the raven are highly efficient individuals who put ideas into practice. They can be dynamic, but they may not always seize opportunities when they arise. Individuals born under this sign are pretty tech-savvy people, so they are able to learn and use the latest technology quite easily, and they can use it to their advantage. They try to achieve a balance in everything, so they tend to sit on the fence, weighing up all the pros and cons of a situation before making a decision. Ravens are very ambitious; they have great potential for new and successful enterprises.

People born under this sign hate discord or conflict and do not take kindly to those who cause trouble. They don't hold grudges, but if someone hurts them, they will not forget it. But they can be very diplomatic, reasonable, and impartial, and they will often do anything for a peaceful life. They are often softly spoken, which can lend authority to anything they say.

THE RAVEN'S POSITIVE TRAITS

People born under the sign of the raven are usually artistic and very diplomatic. They cooperate with others well and can be very forgiving and friendly. They are graceful and refined and like peace and quiet, so you would not see them getting involved in a brawl! Sociable and tactful, if they decide that they like someone, they become lifelong friends. They rarely set out to upset anyone, and they cooperate well with other people. However, they are not as soft as they look, so if they feel that something is wrong, they will stand their ground and ensure that it is done properly and to their rather exacting standards.

THE RAVEN'S NEGATIVE TRAITS

People born under the sign of the raven can be careless and changeable, and they are not the most constant people in relationships. They get bored easily and cannot cope with the demands of others, so they can drift away from their partners quite easily. They are good parents, though, so they rarely abandon their children.

Because they like to weigh the pros and cons of everything, they may appear indecisive and indifferent, but this is only because they feel that they have not had enough time to consider all the options. The personalities of these individuals are not as strong as they appear, so people born under this sign often feel insecure. At times they feel as though they are being pressured to keep up with the rest of the world, when all they want to do is take things at a tried and tested steady pace. They hate doing anything in a hurry. However, there is strength in these people, which shows itself in odd ways. For instance, individuals born under this sign hate injustice and will even put their lives on the line to prevent one from being done.

These individuals can seem to be vain at times, but this is only because they take great pride in their appearance. Later in life, they might be described as "dapper." People born under this sign can come across as superficial. They wonder why people think they are like this, because they cannot see it themselves.

THE RAVEN AND PROFESSION

Individuals born under the sign of the raven are wonderful with people, and they have a pleasant and persuasive manner, so they make great agents and fixers. They can work in sales, but only as long as the job is not too pressured, the business comes in on a regular basis, and they are paid wages with commission, rather than commission only.

They are good at arranging things for other people, so a career as a recruitment consultant, legal adviser, accountant, negotiator, real-estate agent, or counselor would work. They also do well in the beauty industry because they love people to look as good as they do, so a career as a hairdresser, beautician, makeup artist, or masseur is also an ideal choice for people born under this sign.

Many individuals born under the raven sign sing or play musical instruments, and even if they do not, they have such an ear for music that they work in the music industry. A friend of mine who was born under the sign of the raven spent much of his working life selling records and also playing in a band. Some people born under this sign are very artistic and they enjoy meaningful art. Many of them study to be artists and interior designers.

COMPATIBILITY AND THE RAVEN

Being members of the butterfly clan, individuals born under the sign of the raven get along well with other members of the butterfly clan, such as those born under the sign of the otter or the deer. People born under the raven sign are also happy to be with members of the thunderbird clan, such as those born under the sign of the red-tailed hawk, the sturgeon, or the elk.

Famous People Born under the Sign of the Raven

Julie Andrews	John Lennon
Bridget Bardot	Sharon Osborne
Simon Cowell	Luciano Pavarotti
Michael Douglas	Eleanor Roosevelt
T. S. Elliot	Desmond Tutu
Jessie Jackson	Oscar Wilde
Pope John Paul	Catherine Zeta-Jones

18

THE SNAKE
October 24 - November 21

Clan	*Frog*
Spirit keeper	*Spirit Keeper of the West*
Moon	*Freeze-up Moon*
Crystal or mineral	*Copper and malachite*
Tree or plant	*Thistle*
Color	*Orange*

THE FREEZE-UP MOON

The United States is a big place, and the weather varies by region. For instance, the idea of a season when the world starts to freeze makes no sense at all to Native Americans who live in Florida. That said, most Native Americans do not live in tropical areas, so to them, the winter is a reality that they have to prepare for.

When working on a spiritual vibration with the freeze-up Moon, you will learn to become grounded and not too suspicious of other people

THE SNAKE

The snake is a mysterious and magnificent—if somewhat misunderstood—member of the vertebrate family. It has the capacity to travel miles without others hearing it pass by, and it can be quite bold.

Worldwide there are 2,500 different species of snake. In the United States there are only about 250 species and subspecies. Snakes are carnivorous, limbless reptiles that live in a variety of habitats and kill their prey in a variety of ways. Most snakes eat insects and small animals, which makes them useful because they keep the rat and mouse population down. Snakes can adapt well to their environment and are very sensitive. Being cold-blooded, they depend on their environment to keep them warm and safe, especially when they need to hibernate. When they grow too big for their skin, they shed it. When at rest, some snakes change their color to that of their surroundings in order to protect themselves. Some snakes hiss, others, like the rattlesnake, buzz their rattles when they are upset or aware of danger. Despite their reputation, most snakes will attack only in self-defense or for food. Also, courtship between two snakes can be a very warm affair.

The snake is respected in most Native American cultures, as it represents justice and transformation. The Hopi people believe that the snake is a messenger who has the power to bring life-giving rains. The Ojibwa people have a snake clan that specializes in supplying medicinal cures. To them, the snake represents patience, because it is slow to anger. Many Native American peoples used the snake as a symbol of feminine powers and for healing.

Working with the snake can teach you about the mystery and realms of creation. It teaches you to be a better communicator, and it also imparts a spiritual message about the need for self-defense and for protecting your own life force.

THE THISTLE

The thistle is a both a flower and a plant, and all parts of the thistle are rich in minerals. The young stem or root can be eaten raw or cooked, and the fruitlike seeds can be roasted and then used as a cure for stomach and digestive problems, as well as for reducing fever and for strengthening internal organs. Some say that using the thistle in this way increases brain function and makes the brain more active.

The thistle can be used in a meditation to help you contact and understand different levels of reality, to develop healing abilities, and to become less fixed and more versatile.

COPPER AND MALACHITE

Copper and malachite are basically the same mineral, because the beautiful green stone that is malachite contains copper, which is released when malachite is heated in a furnace. Both copper and malachite are said to be able to purify the spirit and the blood when held during a meditation. Native Americans say that copper gives strength, power, and balance, in addition to the ability to understand one's weaknesses and the reasons behind them. Copper's ability to purify blood comes into its own when the metal is worn as a bracelet or an anklet. Those who suffer from rheumatism often find copper bracelets helpful. Malachite has spiritual powers of its own, as it raises a person's sensitivity to the voice of the spirit. It also helps to enhance psychic powers.

When you are working on a spiritual vibration, malachite or copper teaches those born at this time to focus their energies and to become more sensitive to others.

TRAITS OF PEOPLE BORN UNDER THE SIGN OF THE SNAKE

The feelings of people who are born under the sign of the snake can be intense, but these people are also cautious. They avoid revealing their weaknesses to others. On the surface they are bold and confident people, but this facade masks insecurity and a need to protect their feelings. People born under this sign have very powerful personalities that can be a little overwhelming at times, so they must take care not to intimidate others.

Those born under the snake sign have the ability to sum up others at a glance and see right through charlatans almost before they have spoken. The same can be said of a situation, because these people will intuitively know whether it is good or bad. Many are interested in the occult and similar topics, but they like to see these things proved rather than simply take someone else's word for it. Many are excellent strategists, so they will not start out on the road to achievement without thinking things through and having a plan. Life for these individuals is a little like a game—and they like to win!

People born under this sign need to be able to trust those they love and those with whom they live. They also need to be able to trust work colleagues, relatives, and friends. As long as the trust is there, they will do anything for their friends or colleagues. If a friend or colleague does something to lose that trust, though, it will be gone for good.

THE SNAKE'S
POSITIVE TRAITS

People born under the sign of the snake are passionate and determined individuals. When they become devoted to a person or a situation, they are emotional, intense, and intimate. Very loyal and resourceful, these people like to work hard, often getting in to work several hours before anyone else does and getting through a huge workload. They also like to play hard. They are fond of lovemaking and they especially love to travel. They love to throw parties and are wonderful hosts.

Individuals born under the sign of the snake will usually see a situation coming into being long before anything tangible happens, and they are usually proved right. These people are good organizers who can be relied upon to sort things out. They are extremely kind and generous to their friends and to those they love.

THE SNAKE'S NEGATIVE TRAITS

People born under the sign of the snake have extremely hot tempers, and when they have reason to lose their tempers, everybody for miles around had better duck! They are not normally cunning, unless they feel the need to protect their feelings—and then they can ensure that someone else is in the firing line or that someone else takes the flak for them. They can envy others, and they can be moody, jealous, sarcastic, and unforgiving. They can be a little overbearing at times, and it is sometimes wise to tell them in no uncertain terms to go away until they calm down. They can keep an argument going for days if they think they are right.

People born under this sign can have a blind spot when it comes to others, not seeing the effect their words and actions can have on them. They may win every argument by being cutting or insisting that they are right, but sooner or later, people get fed up with this and leave them. At this point, people born under this sign wonder what they did wrong and why their friends, relatives, or neighbors do not like them anymore.

THE SNAKE AND PROFESSION

People born under the sign of the snake will do well in any position of authority and leadership, although they are often happier to be near the top rather than at the pinnacle. Their confidence can evaporate sometimes, and there are occasions when they feel that they cannot trust their own judgment, so having a boss or colleague to talk things over with in confidence with is the ideal solution.

These individuals like to feel valuable to society, and they are very active, so a career in the police force, security service, or fire department, or as a sailor or an intelligence officer suits these people to a T. Many make good surgeons, nurses, and chiropractors or sports trainers. They enjoy anything connected with travel, so they may enjoy working at an airport. Interestingly, a friend of mine who was born under the sign of the snake was once an intelligence officer in the navy, and another works as a security officer in an airport!

People born under this sign love music and may sing or play in a band or work in some aspect of the music industry. Even given this propensity for music, the one job that these individuals excel at above all others is salesmanship. Anything that takes them out and about seeing customers, sorting out their problems, and persuading them to buy things makes people born under this sign very happy.

COMPATIBILITY AND THE SNAKE

People born under the sign of the snake are members of the frog clan, so they are compatible with other members of the frog clan, such as those born under the sign of the cougar or the flicker. They also get along well with members of the turtle clan, such as those born under the sign of the snow goose, beaver, or grizzly bear.

Famous People Born under the Sign of the Snake

Marie Antoinette

Charles Bronson

Charles, Prince of Wales

Marie Curie

Jodi Foster

Bill Gates

Whoopi Goldberg

Katherine Hepburn

John Keats

Robert Kennedy

Demi Moore

Pablo Picasso

Theodore Roosevelt

Winona Ryder

Robert Louis Stevenson

Bram Stoker

Ted Turner

19

THE ELK
November 22 - December 21

Clan	Thunderbird
Spirit keeper	Spirit Keeper of the West
Moon	Long-snows Moon
Crystal or mineral	Obsidian
Tree or plant	Black Spruce
Color	Black

LONG—SNOWS MOON

Most of the United States gets very cold at this time of the year, and it may feel as though winter will go on forever. The solstice on December 21 is a time when many people light candles and say prayers to encourage the Sun to return once again. This is a time for preparing tools and mending teepees or cabins for the following year, but the main activity now is hunting. People who have the elk personality also need to feel free to wander away in search of something interesting whenever the urge takes them.

THE ELK

The elk is the largest and most regal member of the deer family, and its large antlers enhance its stately appearance. The elk lives in the woodlands. They seem to have a sense of responsibility, because when the ground is covered with heavy snow, elks will take turns breaking up the snow to create a trail for others to follow. Elks often prance around or break into a gallop of joy, and can run at speeds of up to thirty miles per hour for short distances.

The elk has few enemies. Cougars, bears, and wolves will sometimes succeed in bringing down a sick or elderly animal, but no animal is a match for a bull in his prime. Before the start of the twentieth century, most elk were slaughtered, and frequently the only reason for killing them was to make two of their teeth into jewels!

Throughout most of the year, the elk, like the deer, live in single-gender herds, but when the mating season begins, males and females mix. Bulls defend their mates from the approach of another bull. In the spring, when it comes time to calve, the cows go to the valleys, and calves are hidden for the first part of their life, so that the mothers can go out and graze. Like fawns, calves are thought to be born without a smell, and this adaptation protects the calves from attracting the interest of predators. Native Americans had a great deal of respect for the elk, primarily for their speed, beauty, and strength.

People born under the sign of the elk need to guard against being overly argumentative and erratic or difficult when in intimate relationships. If you choose to work with the elk on a spiritual level, you will learn about strength, responsibility, joy, speed, and protection. The elk represents insight, independence, and fearlessness.

THE BLACK SPRUCE

The tips of the black spruce's leaves are rich in vitamins, and one can make these leaves into a tea or simply nibble on them. A tea made from black spruce leaves can be used as an antiseptic or for treating the throat and chest. The gum from the black spruce can be applied to cuts and wounds to clean them, and it can also be used as an inhalant.

On a spiritual level, the black spruce can help you connect with the Earth, and it adds to your unique way of reaching "spirit." The black spruce is also linked to the idea of being soft and strong at the same time.

OBSIDIAN

Obsidian is connected with the Earth's energy, as it comes from the inside of volcanoes, so it is a pure product of our planet. It is formed by a fusion of grains of sand and chemicals, which turns the mixture into a kind of black glass.

Large pieces of obsidian were once polished and made into mirrors, and this explains the myth about obsidian being able to reflect or transmit the thoughts of others to the wearer. Obsidian promotes clairvoyance and helps people see into the future, especially when it is used as a "scrying dish," which is used in a similar way to a crystal ball. Obsidian helps people to become more perceptive and to mirror the feelings of others. Obsidian is a strong and protective stone, and if you wear it, it is supposed to be good for clarifying your inner thoughts.

TRAITS OF PEOPLE BORN UNDER THE SIGN OF THE ELK

Individuals who are born under the sign of the elk have a naturally positive outlook on life and are enterprising and full of energy and vitality. Versatile and adventurous, they are eager to expand their range beyond the comfortable and familiar. They enjoy travel and exploring, and their minds are continually searching for new experiences. They are ambitious and optimistic folk, and while they can be self-pitying at times, they are the first to admit that luck is often on their side.

People born under this sign are idealists, and this trait seems to keep them going when they face disappointments. They are believers, and they are willing to fight for their beliefs. They are both loyal and independent, and they manage to balance both traits. Keen students, they are always on the lookout for new experiences. Often intuitive and original thinkers, these individuals are better at adapting than inventing. They work well in collaboration with others.

THE ELK'S POSITIVE TRAITS

People born under the sign of the elk can be generous, resourceful, and caring toward animals. They are ardent and sincere in relationships. Because of their independent nature, they have difficulty maintaining a close personal relationship. They prefer a solid home base, but as a place to return to after they have traveled. They have a compelling need to feel free, and they sometimes make this choice at the expense of their families and friends.

People born under this sign are clever. Some are clever in an academic way, and become experts in a particular subject. All of them are excellent students who can learn extensively and pass exams. Many are highly qualified. All are great teachers, and many of them really settle down in life only when they start to teach. Those who do not have an academic turn of mind are extremely good with their hands. Some are wonderfully innovative dress designers and dress makers, while others can fix, mend, or build anything with little more than a few basic tools in their kit.

Many people born under this sign are charming, and they have a wonderful sense of humor, which encourages others to forgive them a great deal. Some are fascinating and very attractive to the opposite sex.

THE ELK'S NEGATIVE TRAITS

People born under the sign of the elk have quick tempers and often speak without thinking. Their rage may pass as quickly as it started, but their stinging comments are not easily forgotten. They are hypercritical and very quick to point out the inadequacies of others. When they allow their nasty tongue free rein to a child over a period of time, the result is devastating. These people are clever in many ways but extremely stupid in others.

There is a side of individuals born under the sign of the elk that is quite superstitious, and some people take this trait too far. They do not like to be left out of things and they hate secrets. This is mainly because they are self-protective and suspicious, so they tend to think others are cooking up schemes that will be harmful to them. They are not really interested in the feelings and thoughts of others. They can be restless, and their love of freedom can make them unable to stick to anyone or anything.

THE ELK AND PROFESSION

People born under the sign of the elk are natural teachers, so any profession in the teaching or training sector suits them. They thrive on discovery, and they make super scientists. Because they are natural communicators, they do well in any field in which they deal with the public, so law, politics, public service, and social work would be ideal for anyone born under the sign of the elk.

Many work in what used to be called craft trades, such as electrician, carpenter, decorator, and builder. These jobs allow them to take their skills around from place to place, thus avoiding the one thing these people cannot stand, which is to be stuck in the same place day after day.

Many people born under this sign can be found in jobs that allow them to exercise their minds as well as to travel, so many of them work in the field of travel. Some use their quick wit professionally by becoming wonderful comedians.

COMPATIBILITY AND THE ELK

People born under the sign of the elk belong to the thunder-bird clan, so they are compatible with other members of the thunderbird clan, such as those born under the sign of the red-tailed hawk or the sturgeon. They also get along well with members of the butterfly clan, such as those born under the sign of the otter, deer, or raven.

Famous People Born under the Sign of the Elk

Jane Austen	Caroline Kennedy
Ludwig von Beethoven	Bruce Lee
William Blake	Brad Pitt
Winston Churchill	Richard Pryor
Billy Connolly	Frank Sinatra
Walt Disney	Steven Spielberg
Kirk Douglas	Tina Turner
Jane Fonda	Mark Twain

20

TOTEM ANIMALS

Humankind has not woven the web of life.

We are but one thread within it.

Whatever we do to the web,

We do to ourselves.

All things are bound together.

All things connect.

—Chief Seattle

WHAT IS AN ANIMAL TOTEM?

There was a time when we understood that humans were simply a part of the Earth, a small part in the circle of life on Earth. We used to respect nature and we killed only what we ate and used the skins of only what we killed and ate. We did not waste life or disrespect it. There was a time when we gave recognition to the power of the animal spirits by wearing their skins, wearing their images in masks, and honoring them in celebrations.

The natural power of animal totems has not been entirely lost, and many Native American peoples still hold the old beliefs that animals are as important to our survival on Earth as we are. They still believe in the power and knowledge that animal spirits can give us. To live a peaceful and harmonious life, we need to remember that we are not the only animal

Totem Animals: Fox, Segull, Lynx

on this planet, and without other species, be they animal or plant, we would not survive.

An animal totem is in simple terms an animal that we feel connected to. Using animal totems in your life will allow you to become better connected to the Earth, and you will be able to solve life's problems and live a healthier, happier, and more spiritual life. Animals come to us because they have something to teach us, and a particular kind of power they are willing to share with us. Sometimes they provide comfort to us when we need it. They seek to give us the gift of understanding and forgiveness, and they are there to remind us that we are part of the great circle of life and that we should all live in harmony with one another.

Have you ever had a vivid dream in which an animal has played an important role? Animal spirits come to us in our dreams to inform us of something we need to know in order to survive. For example, if you dreamt about a lion, it might be telling you to find inner strength to see you through tough times.

Having an animal totem does not mean that you need to care for that particular animal physically. It means that you have a spiritual and powerful friend to call upon in times of sorrow, stress, or even joy. Just as some people call on their guardian angels, some Native American peoples call upon their animal totems for guidance and security.

Each and every animal has its own special power and message to give to us, because every animal has a powerful spirit and a special skill. Animal spirits tend to choose a person rather than the other way around. You may learn of your totem animal via a dream or through the connection to or love you have for one particular animal, or even from the way you operate or behave. For example, if you are naturally graceful and quiet, you might find that you connect with an animal of similar traits, such as the swan. Remember, the animal will usually choose you.

TYPES OF ANIMAL TOTEMS

When you are looking for your animal totem, it is important to remember that the totem that comes to you is yours for life. It's not real if you decide one week that your animal totem is the great bear and then the next you change it to a swallow! All totems are powerful, but the meaning that yours brings will vary depending on what type of totem has come to you.

Lifelong Animal Totem

The lifelong animal totem stays with you for your entire life. It will always be there when you need it and will always give you its power when you need it most. You may have only one or you may have more than one lifelong totem. Your totem may come into your life at any time. Many people call your lifelong totem your "spirit totem." If for example, your lifelong totem is a penguin, you will be very spiritual. The penguin, which moves better in the water than it does on land, is able to leap out of water; this ability represents the ability to have out-of-body experiences.

Journey Animal Totem

The journey animal totem reflects a period of time, not necessarily just a day, but possibly a few weeks at a time—sometimes a few months or several years. This animal totem is around for the period of time that it takes you to walk the path that the animal totem is guiding you on.

During this journey you will discover that this particular animal totem will show up in your life several times. For instance, you may notice signs of a particular animal on everyday things. If your animal totem is a dove, you might be flipping through a magazine when a picture of a dove catches your eye; then you might be in a store and notice a postcard with a dove on it, or you might receive a phone call from a Mrs. Dove. Don't assume that these experiences are coincidences. They are most likely your animal spirit trying to connect to you through ways it thinks you will notice.

You may find that several animal totems appear in your life to guide you on your path. If one, two, or three animals suddenly make an appearance, notice whether they share certain characteristics, because then you have found the basis of your path. The difference between the journey animal totem and the message animal totem (see the next section) is one of duration. The message animal totem slips in and out of your life quickly, while the journey animal totem remains with you for as long as you need it to help you on that part of your journey.

Message Animal Totem

The message animal totem usually brings growth or a cautionary warning. It is often a wake-up call or a signal that you need to pay attention to. You may go through an unusual experience that makes a very powerful statement at that particular time. A message totem might show up suddenly in the middle of a dream and it may start to talk or impart a message. You should listen to what it has to say. It might be a warning not to buy a certain house or a reassurance about taking a job that you have been offered. The message may forewarn of danger, such as telling you not to travel on a certain road at a certain time of the day, or it may prompt you to phone a certain person who will have important news for you.

Shadow Animal Totem

Shadow animal totems are the ones that test us. They have great power that they can use to help you, but they may put you through tests before they let their power work. In all of nature there is prey and there are predators, and this pairing also exists in the spiritual shadow world. A shadow totem is one you that you might initially fear, so it represents overcoming a particular fear in order to fulfill what you want in life. For example, if you are scared of spiders, and your shadow totem wants to connect with you, you might discover that your house has more spiders in it than usual.

Until you learn to stop screaming the house down for someone to "get the spider out of the bathtub," you will not be in a position to hear what your totem is telling you. So calmly accept that the animal or creature you fear most is also a part of nature, and only when you conquer your fears will you receive your message.

DISCOVERING YOUR ANIMAL TOTEM

Below is a series of questions that will help you to discover your animal totem. You may not have come across your journey or message totems yet, and discovering your animal totem is not always easy. When you look through the questions that follow, you may find that you have more than one answer per question. That's fine; follow your instincts when answering the question, and if you are in any doubt, don't answer it.

Discovering Your Lifelong Animal Totem

- When you were a child, what animal did you collect, observe, or obsess over that you are still attracted to today?

- If you could have any animal as a pet, what would it be?

- When you go to the zoo, which animal are you drawn to or do you spend most of your time with?

- If you could be an animal, what would it be?

- What animal are you afraid of, even if you have no idea why you are afraid of it?

- When you are out, do you often run into the same kind of animal?

- What animal seems to crop up over and over again in your life?

- What animal would you watch for hours?

- What animal most fascinates you?

- Does artwork or jewelry that depicts a certain animal always attract you?

If you mentioned one particular animal in response to at least three of the above-mentioned questions, that animal is your lifelong animal totem.

Discovering Your Journey Animal Totem

- What animal have you started seeing that you have not seen before?

- What new animal are you attracted to?

- Have you been dreaming of an animal lately?

- Have you been thinking about a new animal lately?

- In the past two weeks, what animals have you seen or dreamt of several times?

If you have a journey animal totem, you will have answered at least three of these questions with the same animal. This animal is blessing your path for a reason.

Discovering Your Message Animal Totem

- What animal surprised or startled you today?

- What animal that you don't usually see have you seen a couple of times today?

- What animal entered your house today?

If you answered the same animal for two questions, then this animal is your message totem animal, bringing an important message for you. You should heed what it has to say.

Discovering Your Shadow Animal Totem

- What animal attacks have you been in?

- What scary animal situations have you been in?

- Does a certain animal make you afraid?

- What animals do you run from?

- What animals do you have nightmares about?

- Does just watching television and seeing that animal appear on the screen scare you?

If you answered two questions with the same animal, this means that you have a shadow totem, and you must address the problem. Remember that shadow totems will continue to test you and work against you, and you need to embrace a lesson of the animal totem and conquer your fear for it to disappear again.

MEETING YOUR ANIMAL TOTEM

Your animal totem is the animal that seems to have played an important part in your life ever since childhood. You might love dolphins and have a huge collection of things that are related to dolphins, and if anyone asked you why, you might say, I just like them. In fact, this would be your lifelong animal totem.

Your animal totem has many messages for you, and you can learn what these are by studying everything you can about your animal. The best way to learn about your animal totem is to do as much research as you can on that particular animal. For example:

- Where does it live?

- What does it eat?

- How does it get food?

- What are the physical characteristics of your animal?

- What does it look like?

- What special traits and skills does it have?

- What is its home like?

- Where does it sleep?

- When does it sleep?

- What is its social life like?

- What are its mating habits?

In studying these things you will gain insight into your animal and the meaning it has for you. You might discover that the owl is your animal totem and that you share many traits, such as being a nocturnal person.

HOW TO CALL FOR HELP FROM YOUR ANIMAL TOTEM

You may have to use another method to tune in to your main animal totem, journey totem, message totem, or shadow totem. This method is meditation, and it works.

Native Americans are great believers in meditation, and they use the technique to call upon their animal totems for guidance. Meditation is not as hard as it may sound. It is simply a method of relaxing and letting your mind become completely clear—similar to the experience when you are just drifting off to sleep. With practice you will soon discover that the answers to any problems you may have will come easily to you once you start calling upon your animal totem for guidance.

Here is an extensive list of animals and some traditional ideas that correspond to them. If you don't like the ideas that you find associated with an animal that you are drawn to, use your own feelings about the animal.

Animal	Description
Alligator	Patience, survival, stealth
Ant	Hard work, cooperation, patience
Antelope	Speed, grace, agility, cooperation
Armadillo	Protection, defense
Badger	Aggression
Bat	Group activities
Bear	Strength, power
Beaver	Work, practical applications
Buffalo	Sufficiency, health, luck
Butterfly	Transformation, beauty
Caribou	Patience, travel
Cougar	Magnanimity, grace
Coyote	Slyness, humor, bad luck
Crane	Elegance, balance
Crow	Endurance, wisdom
Deer	Gentleness, sensitivity, grace

Dog	Loyalty, friendship, love
Dolphin	Joy, harmony, connection with spirit
Dove	Peace, love, passion, loyalty
Dragonfly	Beauty, skill, speed
Eagle	Spirit, strength, healing, wisdom
Elk	Stamina, reliability
Fox	Intelligence, slyness, discretion
Frog	Cleansing, peace, healing
Goat	Ambition, diligence
Goose	Fresh starts, assertiveness
Hawk	Understanding, intelligence
Hedgehog	Self-preservation
Horse	Travel, freedom, movement
Hummingbird	Beauty, refinement
Lizard	Sometimes fear, otherwise patience
Lynx	Salesmanship, hunting skills
Moose	Self-esteem
Mouse	Speed, quick-wittedness
Opossum	Ability to keep secrets

Otter	Women, happiness, laughter
Owl	Wisdom
Porcupine	Security, safety
Rabbit	Cleverness, ability to survive anything
Salmon	Strength, determination
Seagull	Hunting skills, freedom
Seal	Friendliness
Skunk	Treachery, scandal
Snail	Protection, perseverance
Snake	Sexuality, transformation, reincarnation
Spider	Diligence, connections
Squirrel	Thrift, ability to save money
Swan	Elegance, relationships, beauty
Turkey	Abundance
Turtle	Love, healing, knowledge
Whale	Intuition, travel, keeper of records
Weasel	Stealth
Wolf	Creativity, intuition, teaching ability

index